Xmo

Fail-Safe
Investing

Also by Peter Nagan

The Medical Almanac

FAIL-SAFE INVESTING

How to Make Money with Less than $10,000!

Peter Nagan

G. P. Putnam's Sons
New York

Library of Congress Cataloging in Publication Data

Nagan, Peter.
  Fail-safe investing.

  1. Investments—Handbooks, manuals, etc.
I. Title.
HG4527.N34   1981   332.6′78   81-1208
ISBN 0-399-12616-3   AACR2

PRINTED IN THE UNITED STATES OF AMERICA

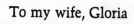

To my wife, Gloria

CONTENTS

An Introduction to Fail-Safe Investing   9

SECTION I — *BEFORE YOU TAKE THE PLUNGE*
CHAPTER ONE: *A Dissent on Doomsday*   17
CHAPTER TWO: *What Kind of Investor Are You?*   23
CHAPTER THREE: *How to Design an Investment Plan*   29
CHAPTER FOUR: *The Investment Climate of the Eighties*   35

SECTION II — *INCOME (AND SAFETY) FIRST*
CHAPTER FIVE: *Life Insurance Before All Else*   45
CHAPTER SIX: *Savings for a Rainy Day*   51
CHAPTER SEVEN: *The Why and How of Fixed-Income Securities*   57
CHAPTER EIGHT: *U.S. Treasury Obligations*   75
CHAPTER NINE: *Federal-Agency Issues*   89
CHAPTER TEN: *Tax-Exempt State and Local Government Securities*   97
CHAPTER ELEVEN: *Corporate Bonds and Notes*   107
CHAPTER TWELVE: *Other Short-Term Investments*   115

SECTION III — *SOME MORE RISK FOR MORE PROFIT*
CHAPTER THIRTEEN: *Common Stocks*   123
CHAPTER FOURTEEN: *Real Estate*   139

CHAPTER FIFTEEN: *Real-Estate Securities*   157
CHAPTER SIXTEEN: *Other Tax Shelters*   165

Glossary of Tax-Shelter Terms and Provisions   181

SECTION IV — *SPECULATING INSTEAD OF INVESTING*
CHAPTER SEVENTEEN: *Gold, Silver, and Diamonds*   185
CHAPTER EIGHTEEN: *Commodities*   197
CHAPTER NINETEEN: *Collectibles*   205
CHAPTER TWENTY: *Scams and Cons*   209

SECTION V — *GETTING GOOD ADVICE*
CHAPTER TWENTY-ONE: *Whom Can You Trust?*   223

AN INTRODUCTION
TO FAIL-SAFE INVESTING

The title of this book was chosen with great care. It telegraphs the principles—the strategies—that should enable you to profit handsomely from your investments in the years ahead while minimizing the risks of loss of your capital.

Fail-Safe Investing won't tell you how you can run a shoestring into a fortune with nothing but a simple, little-known formula. It won't show you how to survive—and prosper from—the catastrophes that some authors confidently predict will engulf us all in the years just ahead.

Rather, *Fail-Safe Investing* is designed as a guide for those who have accumulated a "nut" and now want—above all—to preserve it and its real worth or buying power from foolish mistakes or the inroads of inflation. With that assured, these investors want to make as much money as they possibly can in income and capital gains. Many of these men and women have learned the hard way that, all too often, the bigger the promised profit, the bigger the risk involved. Having been burned in the past when forecasts didn't turn out as expected, or when they took the wrong advice, they don't want to take chances with money that is earmarked

for important things like a home, education, retirement or
their children's inheritance.

This isn't to say that these people must be content with
staid blue-chip stocks, savings certificates at banks or savings and loan associations or the popular money-market mutual funds; such items do have their place in anyone's investment program at certain times. But there are other, often more rewarding investments that still don't require taking big chances. There are no carefully guarded secrets involved; most of these approaches are well-known to professional money managers who guide the destinies of big financial institutions. But a vast number of people have never
heard of many of these opportunities; they are too busy
making a living to have become experts at managing money. Or, if they have heard about these possibilities, they
tend to believe that only the wealthy—the smart-money
types—know how to turn them to advantage.

These are the people that *Fail-Safe Investing* is designed to
serve.

First—it can help by pointing out that it isn't true that
only the rich can capitalize on high-yielding investments or
benefit from programs that keep principal and income
growing faster than inflation.

Second—it can tell you how to go about designing an
investment program that will achieve your goals, while providing for the security of your family.

Third—it will try to spell out in layman's terms the
specifics of many investments that may have seemed mysterious and complicated . . . that is, to answer the questions that you didn't know whom to ask.

Fourth—*Fail-Safe Investing* will try to steer you away
from the many pitfalls and booby traps that litter the path
of the unwary—of big-money people as well as new and
small-scale investors. It will point out the schemes to stay
away from, as well as the investments to consider. There
may be as many no-no's as green lights.

Fifth—it will be reasonable and realistic. You won't
have to suspend belief and enter a fantasy world of magic

formulas or overwhelming calamity in order to accept the
author's conclusions or follow his approach.

Many people like to read about building a fortune. In the
back of their minds there is always the small hard-to-put-
down hope that maybe—just maybe—this or that promoter
really has the answer this time. It can be a harmless pas-
time—as long as it isn't taken too seriously and doesn't
move you to take advice without the most careful and critical review.

The get-rich-quick approach is simply not the way to
safe, successful investing. Hard-boiled financial professionals don't let themselves be deluded by pie-in-the-sky when
it comes to investments that determine the bottom line of
profit and loss. And neither should you.

So you won't find the stuff of dreams of instant wealth in
the pages that follow. Most people know, deep down, that in
this world rewards are not to be had merely for the wishing.
Except for those lucky enough to inherit it, wealth is usually the result of years of hard work, a lot of common sense—
and some luck, too. Many of the investments to be discussed
are available in units of sale of $1,000 and sometimes small-
er; the minimums will be noted as we go along. Regardless
of the size of your initial commitment, though, you would
be able in some cases to earn yields of 20% or more annually, and still avoid taking major risks.

As we'll point out later on, you can't expect to avoid risk
entirely; there is always some element of chance involved
in investing—as there is in every sort of human endeavor.
Even Treasury bonds have a certain kind of exposure to
loss—though less than any other financial asset. But this
book will lay major stress on ways of minimizing risk. At
the head of each chapter on specific investments, we'll rate
the vehicles for the degree of risk they carry. You will still
have to look both ways before you step off the curb, but you
won't find yourself crossing the Grand Canyon on a tight-
rope, either.

In short, and here is the nub of it, *Fail-Safe Investing* is for
people who are conservative where their finances are con-

cerned. It focuses on *investing*, with the term understood to mean committing funds for assured, longer-term growth of capital as well as for obtaining steady income. But, *speculating*—taking high risks in hopes of high, relatively short-term profits—is assumed here to be unwise and contrary to the interests of most investors.

To be sure, people like to take a flyer now and then—a ticket on a state lottery, a gamble on a horse, or maybe a flutter in a "hot" stock. There is an undeniable thrill in watching how it all turns out—in waiting to see whether your judgment is being vindicated. And there is no harm in it if you measure your potential loss carefully and are certain that you can afford to take it.

But speculation should never be confused with the serious business of investing your money for the highest returns that are consistent with a high degree of safety. You won't make killings by prudent investing, but you won't lie awake nights worrying, either.

The various chapters will tell you, systematically and in detail, what to invest in to make the most money (with the least risk) and how to do it. For the most part, you'll find very few predictions of the future. Essentially, it is the aim of this book to pinpoint the investment vehicles that will be most rewarding for you, even as economic conditions change. In the process, *Fail-Safe Investing* will range over the entire array of opportunities that our financial system affords, explaining how they work, how they may—or may not—meet your needs, and the degree of risk involved.

In essence, *Fail-Safe Investing*'s philosophy can be stated very simply:

- ***Shun the long shots*** and be content with long-term results (though be ready to dump a poor performer at any time or to take an unexpectedly large profit).
- ***Be wary of long-term fixed-income investments*** in this inflationary era. Rewards can still be worthwhile, but timing of purchases—at just the right stage of the cycle—is absolutely critical.

> • *Make the core of your holdings properly chosen real estate and the right kind of common stocks.*
> • *Stay away from commodities and collectibles.*
> • *Approach such exotics as gold and diamonds with the greatest skepticism—* if at all.

But helping you develop an effective investment philosophy is only one of *Fail-Safe Investing*'s two major aims. The other is to provide a sort of concise "encyclopedia" that defines and explains many of the technical complexities of the investment opportunities we will be dealing with. You may already understand the mechanics of the bond market, stock options, and tax shelters. But just in case there are aspects you haven't come across, we'll be weaving the essentials of these and many other subjects into our discussions in every chapter.

Now—for the way this book is structured. To start, there's a section of several chapters that can help you define what you want your investments to do for you, plus some steps that should be taken before you sign the first check. Then, we'll look at the likely economic climate in which you will be making your investment decisions in the Decade of the Eighties. After that, all about interest rates and yields and the whole array of fixed-income securities, starting with the very safest—those issued by the U.S. Treasury—and working through to other types. You will learn how these issues are marketed, where they can be purchased and sold in amounts you will most likely find suitable; how you can keep up with their prices; how often they pay dividends or interest; and the tax advantages an investment may or may not offer.

Next, we'll examine the various kind of equity situations—common stocks and real estate—and wind up with a section on the sort of things you should avoid, either because they are so very risky or because they are outright frauds. There's also a chapter on how to get the best invest-ment advice if you think you need it.

You'll quickly discover that *Fail-Safe Investing* is not a gloom-and-doom book. It assumes that the earth will contin-ue to spin on its axis for a long time to come—and that you can count on this in making your investment decisions.

Most people have to face problems in the years ahead that won't be all that different from those obtaining now— excessively high inflation, uncomfortably high taxes, and a recurrent business cycle. But you won't have to dig a fox-hole and hunker down. There are ways to invest—safe ways that often can be effectuated by a telephone call to a broker—that will pay off handsomely and still let you sleep soundly at night. The pages that follow will tell you how.

SECTION I

BEFORE YOU TAKE THE PLUNGE

CHAPTER ONE

A DISSENT ON DOOMSDAY

At the very start, it should be clearly understood that this book does not subscribe to the Doomsday theory of investing. You won't be urged to buy gold and diamonds or the other favorites of those who insistently proclaim that calamity will befall us all a few short years hence. By going along with this book's stance you may miss opportunities to profit—but you may also avoid substantial losses.

The theme of the Doomsayers is largely the same: The country—and the world—are in sad shape and are deteriorating rapidly all the time. Little groups of willful men in Washington (and Wall Street, too) are consciously or otherwise making decisions to bankrupt the country and its industry, debase its currency, and wipe out all your wealth. In a very short time—perhaps two or three years hence—the economic and social fabric of the nation will come apart. Ronald Reagan's election may slow the process—but not very much, really. Under the gloom-and-doom scenario, revolution and anarchy will follow an overall economic breakdown. However, those who take what the conventional wisdom says are outlandish precautions will survive general ruin.

Each of the prophets of disaster has his own variation of the basic scenario that outlines how Armageddon will come about. Some say that it will be a Great Depression to be brought on in some way by a decline in living standards. Others predict that most wealth will be obliterated by a catastrophic collapse in currency values. The more "conservative" forecast a roughly similar end-result, developing over a somewhat longer span of years, from an accelerating rate of inflation that ultimately will resemble Germany's after World War I.

In essence, what they all are selling is fear. They play on the human hunger to know the future and the need to be assured that, no matter what happens, the individual will survive. Talk of overwhelming danger and disaster touches a nerve in everyone.

With most persons, those needs and fears are reasonable and are kept in perspective. Many can tolerate—even enjoy—a good scare, if it isn't too intense. Remember the delicious thrills of your own childhood, as you and your playmates frightened yourselves with tales of ghosts and horror. And note the popularity of movies about catastrophes— portraying the terror of those caught in a capsized superliner, a burning skyscraper, a California earthquake, or an invasion by aliens from outer space. For most, an extra shot of adrenaline now and then does little harm.

But some others take their fears of calamity much more seriously—in some cases, perhaps, to the point of paranoia. They may constitute only a small percentage of the investing population, but are a substantial group in absolute number. Most could be labeled middle class or even moderately wealthy—comfortable, conservative, and convinced that the have-nots and do-gooders are out to appropriate their property. They are nervous, apprehensive, and desperate to know what's going to happen and what to do. Even those who have done well, but not as well as they think they should have, are dissatisfied with much in the present order of things. The Establishment is to blame; it is running their world into the ground, trampling on their cherished values in the process. Some observers see a similarity to the stirrings of fundamentalist religious groups, which seek to cleanse today's permissive society of its corruption and go back to an era in which the Puritan virtues are re-enshrined.

A number of evangelists have risen to minister to this gloomy group. They counsel their investor-flocks in books, newsletters, personal high-fee sessions and increasingly popular seminars. Some of the faithful follow a circuit, attending one-, two-, or three-day meetings in Miami, New Orleans, Los Angeles, New York, and other major cities; as many as 1,000 at a time pay up to $400 or $500 apiece—with the entire trip tax deductible as an aid to maintaining or increasing investment—to hear their leaders reveal the truth.

Many of these light-bringers are talented pitchmen who speak with fervor and possess a hypnotic talent to sway a crowd while their assistants are passing down the aisles distributing subscription forms to their various services. The Doomsayers' backgrounds are varied. Some have come out of Wall Street firms. Others drifted from one abortive or failed enterprise or another until they found the secret of making money. (Indeed, past failures are a sales asset: "Nothing went right until I suddenly realized . . .") A few come from comfortable, even wealthy families, but cannot be satisfied with annual returns of only 15% or 20%.

To a man, they deny indignantly that they are exploiting their followers' fears for the greater glory of their own bank accounts. To the contrary—they insist that they are helping their clients pierce the smokescreens of misinformation thrown up by government officials, business leaders, and conventionally minded financial analysts. First, they confirm their listeners' darkest fears of catastrophe, using economic reasoning that sounds all the more plausible because it has so little relevance to the prevailing wisdom. Then, they promise to show the true believer their own exclusive Royal Roads to Riches—their special, private formulas for making big-time money—or, increasingly, to save what you have when the Deluge comes and everyone else loses all he possesses.

It doesn't seem to matter to the investor who travels across the country to attend a symposium of leading Doomsayers that the advice of the second speaker contradicts that of the first. The differences can be dismissed as matters of detail—of particular preference—rather than of underlying philosophy. In many cases, the attendees are already convinced of the validity—the truth—of what they hear before they hear it. They come to be reassured—not really to learn whatever may be new in what the speakers have to say.

With a few exceptions, what the speakers have to say boils down to this:

> • *Sell your real estate and your stocks and bonds.*
> • *Put the proceeds into gold, silver, and diamonds,* keeping some in your bedroom and the rest in vaults in Switzerland, Hong Kong, and Canada; some would add to the list gold shares, and a house in the country that's stocked with guns and a year's supply of food and water.

It is very hard to argue with the Doomsayers' reasoning. In their view, to point out that a calamity that was supposed to strike in 1979 has not occurred yet is to quibble over a date. Some claim to have been highly successful in following their own advice to buy gold, silver, and diamonds. It may be hard to confirm such claims. But it is clear that many have struck it big in selling those methods to an eager public.

But this book disagrees with their forecasts of the future and the courses of action they recommend.

This is not to say that this country doesn't have serious problems—and plenty of them: Inflation, recurrent recessions, instability abroad, and a standard of living that has been flat in recent years. But there never was a time when there weren't clouds on the horizon, some of them as dark as today's. One doesn't have to claim that this is the best of all possible worlds to conclude that the Doomsayers' forecasts are exaggerated to say the least and maybe a little paranoid.

For one thing, the country is politically stable. The election of 1980 was convincing proof of that. There were far worse riots in the Sixties and mid-Seventies than seem likely to flare up now.

For another, inflation seems to have settled in at a rate of 10% or so. That's not good or healthy. It enervates the economy and distorts the process of decision-making. But the rise in the price indexes isn't likely to accelerate — it certainly won't be anything like the German inflation in the Twenties.

Real incomes haven't plunged in an alarming way. They haven't grown much in recent years, to be sure, but the stagnation isn't so painful as to touch off social unrest. There has been grumbling in, say, the steel and automaking industries but — considering the sweep of the technological adjustments going on in this country — it has not been all that much. Over all, the country is keeping warm, eating well, and living comfortably.

Look at it this way: To follow the Doomsayers is to bet that this country and its world trading partners are finished as viable economic powers. You would be betting that the malaise of the Seventies is the flavor of the future, instead of being merely a ten-year adjustment period in a two-century perspective of growth and progress. The alternative thesis is that the Viet Nam War and its inflationary aftermath did, in fact, blight and dishearten the country for a decade; but now the malaise is fading, if slowly, and the material resources and human skills that this country possesses in such overwhelming abundance are beginning to re-emerge as an economic force. This country has some readjusting to do — to the fact that other nations have developed powerful competitive economies, and also that American industrial strength is shifting away from heavy industry to high technology.

But the shift is in gear. The period of high inflation and lagging growth is probably not over yet, but the country will soon be moving again at a better pace. You don't have to be a superpatriot to believe this. Just don't be quick to suspect the worst.

Even if the country isn't going to the dogs, aren't gold and diamonds still a good investment? Didn't they outperform just about every other type of asset in the Seventies? The answer is no. To begin with, gold, silver, diamonds and the like aren't investments. They don't possess any income-earning capability. Rather, they are speculations. Maybe that's a quibble over words; who should care what you call it, if the value of the asset has increased more than twenty-fold, as gold did between the middle of 1971 and early 1980?

But the fact is that these items represent risky speculations, despite the spectacular gains of the past decade. We'll develop this theme more fully in Chapter Seventeen.

Remember those newspaper stories of the religious families who disposed of all their goods and waited for the world to end on the date—long since past—that their leader prophesied? Some of them may still be waiting—but without their real estate, stocks, and bonds. There's more at stake in following the Doomsayers' lead than just losing sleep: You could lose much—maybe all—of what you own.

CHAPTER TWO

WHAT KIND OF INVESTOR ARE YOU?

Many investors will fail to take full advantage of the opportunities of the Eighties—not because of inexperience or bad luck, but because they simply haven't developed investment approaches—philosophies, really—that take full account of their personalities and ways of thinking as well as a sound set of principles. Each person's emotional make-up and temperament influences how and where he decides to commit his money.

Some people are out-and-out gamblers. They dream of making a killing in a hot new technology or penny oil stock with only a little stake to start with. Often, it's the sheer excitement of waiting for the outcome that leads them into unsound flyers—alluring get-rich-quick, long-shot deals that pile up loss after loss; in some cases, it's an escape from humdrum lives. They may shift their focus from time to time—from stocks to real estate to gold, etc.—but they are always speculators, in and out for the short term.

Others are simply young, new to the "game," and impatient to make it big. They can't merely settle for high income, or a mix of income and moderate capital gains—the

kind of investments that a professional adviser would suggest. They are aggressive. They want to double their money
on the big score and, confident in their own judgment, will
take chances that, often as not, will cut into their usually
limited capital and even perhaps their rainy-day reserves.
Thus, they look with favor on, say, new stocks with a big
growth potential—but with just as big a chance of losing
out in the scramble for success. In a nutshell, they are
inclined to take risky flyers, trusting to luck to validate
their decisions. Fortunately, it's a predilection that fades as
they grow older.

*Still another group goes to the opposite ex-
treme.* They are intensely conservative—depression ba-
bies who have never gotten over the traumas of bond defaults, home foreclosures, and long periods of a father's unemployment. They will go to any lengths to avoid the
slightest risk. Such persons are prone to seek out government-insured, fixed-income assets, despite the fact that the
value of these assets is constantly being eroded by inflation.
Indeed, they shouldn't be called investors at all; they are
really savers.

However, many have a balanced view. They
are willing to take a limited amount of risk—occasionally
on a long shot with the potential of a Xerox or IBM—to get
appreciably higher returns on their money. Sure, they'd
like to make a killing but, even more, they want their exposure to be prudent and clearly understood. They tend to be
older and to invest more for the longer pull with less concern about day-to-day fluctuations. Experience has shown
that they are likely to be the most successful.

It's important to know which type you are.
You have to probe for and recognize your own inclinations.
If you are calm and unemotional about the financial decisions you make, there is one less hurdle that you have to
surmount on the way to successful investment results. If
you are a long-shot player, you will have to learn to curb
those carefree impulses—perhaps by seeking help and advice from investment experts while shutting your ears to

tipsters even among your friends and relatives. On the other hand, the squirrel types will have to steel themselves to venture out into a (to them) scary world of alternate opportunities for making money. In other words, it's important to realize whether you tend to be unduly swayed by greed or the need for excitement on the one hand or fear on the other. You don't want to take risks that keep you up nights, but you don't want to pass up chances to make money, either.

This isn't to suggest that you may have to see a psychiatrist in order to improve your investment batting average. But, if you haven't done so before, you'll find it well worth your while to take a little time to reflect on the type of investor you really are.

To begin with, you might ask yourself, bluntly, do you have what it takes to turn $1,000 into $2,000,000 by investing in real estate (or stocks or what have you). It has been done, and no doubt it can be done again, though it gets harder all the time. But it requires a certain kind of personality to pull it off — acquisitive, aggressive, single-minded. Most people aren't like that — and don't want to be. They don't feel that they can focus all their energies on learning all there is to know about a narrow, highly specialized field. Nor would they feel comfortable, and be able to sleep at night, if they had to make the tough decisions that are necessarily involved. Many really don't believe that it would pay off — for them, anyway.

Maybe you are that type — and that's fine. But if you are not, you will be better off acknowledging the fact early on. For the vast majority, the most suitable role is that of the passive investor — a person who doesn't run the business or the venture, but who puts up a share of the money to finance it in return for a share of the earnings and often the tax advantages.

Once you have decided that you are a passive investor, though, there are still some questions to be settled before you are clear about the path you will want to follow. The answers can help you decide, specifically, the kind of investment vehicles with which you will be most comfortable. For example:

Are you really prepared to consider what may be (to you) new, unknown and exotic-sounding types of investments?

> Admittedly, this involves stepping over a threshold that many find hard to cross—even though many they know have done so with gratifying results.

Are you reasonably optimistic that this country and the world will survive in something like its present form over, say, the Decade of the Eighties?

> If so, then you will tend to favor more conventional types of investments, rather than the Doomsday kind.

Do you like to make all your own decisions, or do you feel the need for help from individuals or institutions that you can trust?

> There's no need for hesitation if you don't feel happy carrying the load entirely by yourself. You still face choices, though, as to what kind of help, in what areas, and where to seek it.

Do you have the patience to deal with detail—in digging into an investment situation, keeping records, and analyzing data?

> If not, maybe you shouldn't try. You can turn more or less of the task over to professional managers—for fees, of course.

Have you closed your mind to particular possibilities because of what has happened to you—or what you heard has happened to others—in the past? Do you assume that entire classes of investments have nothing to offer you?

> That could be a big mistake. Times—and the risks involved—do change. Each situation should be judged on its present merits.

You shouldn't, for example, automatically rule the stock market out of your investment approach because you fear that, someday, there will be a repeat of the Crash of 1929 when so many were wiped out. Nor should you be put off because it took so long for the Dow-Jones Industrials Average to rescale the peak of 1052 reached in January 1973. These days there are governmental and other safeguards against the excesses that hurt so many investors—perhaps really speculators—a half-century ago. A prudent, well-conceived approach to stocks can yield excellent results with a high degree of safety.

Conversely, no investor should place his faith blindly in "riskless" investments, such as those guaranteed by the full faith and credit of the Federal government or insured by one of its agencies. Such vehicles may still have a role to play in your investment program; that role will be outlined with precision in some of the chapters that follow. But the current high rates of inflation call for a whole new way of looking at these securities.

And you should not conclude in advance that real estate is too ambitious and/or complex an area for your participation. You would be right in respecting the pitfalls that abound, and the demands on your time and judgment that it could generate. But this book will show you ways by which you can limit your commitment of time and money to ones with which you will feel comfortable.

CHAPTER THREE

HOW TO DESIGN
AN INVESTMENT PLAN

As a prelude to discussing specific investments, you ought to design a broad, over-all investment or estate plan. This doesn't mean estate in the sense of the property you'll be leaving to your heirs but, rather, all the things you own now or would like to own and get benefits from in the years ahead, while you are still around to enjoy them. In other words, a comprehensive strategy for allocating your money to various investments or assets in ways that will achieve your objectives.

Those objectives will, of course, vary from individual to individual, if only in the emphasis on certain goals. For the most part, the different plans will be made up of some or all of a list of similar basic elements, but in different proportions. Thus, everyone will want high income, large capital gains, and the flexibility to adjust to changes in interest-rate trends, as well as low risk of loss of principal.

Unfortunately, it's hard to lay down precise rules because no two situations are exactly alike. The tilt of a young family just starting out will be different from that of a person in his or her middle, high-earning years, and still different from someone who has

actually retired. The circumstances of one young family —
or couple in retirement — won't be the same as the similar
household down the street. And the indicated asset mix
would be different for a couple with a large nest egg than it
would be for people who start out with very little. It would
be nice to have hard numerical guidelines to follow — such
and such a percentage in stocks, another for bonds, still
another for real estate. But only you can know the aims and
means of your particular situation.

> You can start out with a stake that's a lot smaller than
> you might think. Many a hefty portfolio or retirement
> nest egg has grown out of the equivalent of less than
> $10,000 even in today's inflated dollars. Certainly, an
> initial fund of $5,000 or $6,000 could get you off to a
> good start. Of course, the more you have to put into a
> single investment, the cheaper your commission ex-
> penses per dollar of capital. But many notes and bonds
> come in units of only $1,000 and there are ways to
> avoid the commissions. Or the fledgling investor can
> start out buying only one or two stocks, adding to the
> number as time goes on and regular set-asides out of
> income expand his investment fund. The principles
> involved are essentially the same.

The elements from which investment plans are typically
constructed will include:

- Your home(s)
- Savings accounts
- The full array of short- and long-term fixed-income
  securities
- Equities — that is, common stocks
- Real estate and real-estate securities
- Ordinary life insurance or annuities
- Pension, Social Security, and profit-sharing benefits
- Gold, silver, and other commodities
- Antiques, rare stamps, and other collectibles

To begin with, investors of all ages and sit-uations should keep funds in quickly accessible form for use in case of emergency. (See Chapter Six for the kinds that may suit your needs.)

How much to keep in liquid form? Enough to meet your family's needs for, say, a month or two—or for as long as you think it might take to liquidate other assets or receive a life-insurance payment. Some prudent advisers suggest that a minimum of $4,000 or $5,000 be kept in ready-at-hand form.

For a young adult with an adequate current income and no dependents or immediate prospects of having any, the emphasis should be on investments that downplay current income in favor of future growth of assets.

This suggests owning, in one way or another, common stocks of companies that pay small dividends in order to conserve cash to plow back into expansion and growth. (It doesn't mean, though, that you should shun the big solid companies in favor of new and highly speculative issues.) Consider a "starter" home, too.

For the young family, the first concern has to be the protection of dependents—that is, an assured income that, together with survivors' benefits under Social Security, will see the children through to maturity and the spouse— more likely in the case of a woman—provided for beyond that.

So a life insurance policy becomes the first priority. (See Chapter Five for the right kind.) After that, a rainy-day fund. Then a home, with its tax-cutting and inflation-fighting advantages, should be considered. Common stocks, too, with what you have left to invest. Fixed-income securities should have a relatively low priority.

For the person in the "prime," high-earning years, the emphasis shifts more heavily to pre-retirement considerations—building the estate that will provide the financial security and comfort for the time when earned income drops or stops altogether.

> The amount of life insurance could well remain fairly substantial, with the greater need to protect the surviving spouse against the inroads of inflation offset, to a larger or smaller degree, by the reduced necessity to provide for older children. The right kind of growth stocks should continue to claim a relatively large share of assets—perhaps 50%. But real estate should become increasingly important for its tax-sheltering and capital-gains benefits. Because inflation will erode the value of fixed-income securities, they should continue to play a minor role. Depending on your bracket, tax shelters should become increasingly important to reduce the liability for current income.

For those in retirement, current income becomes a prime consideration. As a rule of thumb, you might assume that you'll need two-thirds to four-fifths of your pre-retirement income to let you maintain a roughly similar standard of living. A private pension and/or your Social Security benefits will provide part of that, and your Social Security benefits payments will be tax free. (Congress and the President will keep benefits coming, even if they have to dip into general Treasury revenues to make up shortfalls in payroll-tax collections.) What's more, your benefits will be "indexed" to inflation—that is, increased annually to keep in fairly close track with the rise in the cost of living.

> But fixed-income securities—taxable or tax-exempt, depending on your bracket—will now have a definite role to play—especially types maturing in a year or less. You'll need the greater income-assurance that savings certificates or, say, Treasury issues can provide—

enough invested in this way to provide the income you'll want to live on. Real estate and common stocks, by definition, offer no guarantees. There may still be a place for some stocks, but their nature should change—to higher-yielding issues, rather than those that will pay off largely in capital gains later on. The case for further acquisition of real estate will diminish, unless your bracket continues to make tax shelter important. Real-estate securities may be something else again, if they are the kind that can ultimately be sold in a viable market, should you or your estate require cash. The need for life insurance would decline further, though some term ought to be retained, especially while it still can be renewed at affordable rates.

You'll notice that there is no reference to gold, silver, diamonds, antiques, or other collectibles in these suggestions for investment mixes. One reason for the omission: As already suggested, they do not belong in a conservative investor's portfolio, except under special circumstances. The question will be pursued in detail in later chapters.

Some other general guidelines to keep in mind, regardless of what specific type of investment you are considering:
• ***Determine on a specific amount of money to invest*** at any given time—a figure related to your income or growth objectives and what you can set aside. If possible, try to add to it in regular amounts at regular intervals. Don't be quick to increase the total allotted—say, by drawing cash from your rainy-day fund—because the initial investments have done so well and you'd like to "double up." Similarly, don't be quick to sell out because of interim disappointments that may be related to a passing phase of the overall cycle.
• ***But don't hang on to an investment*** that isn't working out the way you projected—and isn't likely to. Admittedly, it is sometimes hard to distinguish between a temporary downdraft that isn't related to your asset's inherent worth and a change in its specific prospects. Don't,

though, let a refusal to admit a mistake or a sentimental attachment to a security or piece of property keep you from biting the bullet when the time comes.

• **Get professional advice or management** of your funds if you don't want to do your own research or deal with buyers or sellers. You can get it at a reasonable cost by buying mutual funds of one kind or another. Or you can line up an investment adviser. (See the concluding section on how to get professional help.)

• **Build an inflation factor of as much as 10% a year** into your calculations of the income you'll need at any given time. In other words, assume that you'll need 10% more in income every year.

• **Diversify among, as well as within, different types or classes of investments** to spread what risks may still lurk in even the most carefully chosen vehicles. This won't always be possible if you are starting out with a small amount of capital. But as it grows you ought to branch out into a half dozen or so different types — and maybe a few more, if you can keep an attentive eye on them.

• **Don't be tempted to try for a quick killing.** There are opportunities to make large profits on relatively small investments that will come your way from time to time. But remember — the risk will almost always be commensurate with the prospect for gain. And most long shots turn out to be, literally, too good to be true.

• **Don't expect to buy a stock or bond or a piece of property** at its absolute low or to sell it at its all-time high. Move in or out when you think the time is right. Be satisfied with the reasonable profit you expected and don't overstay.

• **And don't let your investments become a mental burden**—a source of worry and concern. If you feel that you are exposed to more risk than you can live with comfortably, cut your commitment down to a level that you can sleep with — or say no to the proposition in the first place. On the other hand, don't be so comfortable with your holdings that you go for long stretches without re-examining them in the light of new developments.

CHAPTER FOUR

THE INVESTMENT CLIMATE
OF THE EIGHTIES

Before getting into the specifics of bonds, stocks, real estate, and the other investment possibilities that we'll be examining and evaluating in later chapters, let's try to sketch the kind of world in which you'll be living—and making your financial decisions—over, say, the next five or ten years. How fast will the economy grow? How bad will inflation be? Where will the growth be centered? The answers will provide the framework for the decisions you will have to make as to where you should be putting your money for the best returns consistent with safety.

No one can provide those answers with precision. Certainly, the country's top economists, with all their sophisticated techniques and computers, have not done all that well in calling the shots over the past decade; they couldn't foresee the huge oil-price increases and their inflationary impact—or the public's unprecedented response thereto. We live in an interrelated world of vast uncertainties where sudden disasters in the Middle East or a poor crop on Russia's collective farms can disrupt vital food, fuel, and other supplies and precipitate dangerous international crises. And even if we should luck out and escape major destabilizing occurrences, there can be no certainty that the most carefully prepared forecasts will hit the mark; the state of the economist's art is not as advanced as many practitioners would like it to be. In other words, long-range predictions have to be read with a high degree of caution — if not with outright skepticism.

Nevertheless, drawing on the expertise of specialists in different areas of economics and political science, we can at least try to indicate some of the basic influences that will dominate the Decade of the Eighties. Actually, it won't be a set of predictions as much as a series of assumptions of what seems logical and reasonable, given what has been happening and what little we can see on the horizon. And it will all be seasoned with a dash of intuition acquired from reporting on and analyzing past cycles as well as developing trends. In the light of this general overview, it should be possible to lay down some broad guiding principles for investment.

One thing you can count on is that the **world of the Eighties will be an era of rapid, often disruptive change.** The primary forces will be heavily political, but the economic implications will be far-reaching as well. The transition to an energy-short world is still in the process of completion. The instabilities in the Middle East, in Southeast Asia, in much of Africa, and in parts of Latin America have yet to give way to relatively lasting regimes and power groupings. And every upheaval will have its ripple — or wave — effect on the U.S.

The malaise that has afflicted the U.S. and some of the other advanced affluent nations over the past decade will dissipate slowly; economic gains will remain moderate. This country, bedeviled by a sense of technical crisis — from low productivity, pollution, and the dangers of nuclear energy — may have passed its peak growth rate; though President Reagan and his advisers hope that their policies will restore the vitality of the past, 3% a year may be more characteristic of the next ten years, after an average of 5% over the last twenty-five.

By contrast, Japan and nations of the Asian Rim will experience growth of 5% and as much as 10% a year. South

Korea and Taiwan, for example, will become members of the industrialized countries' club. Parts of Latin America will be knocking at the door — Brazil, Mexico, and Venezuela. And Portugal, Spain, Yugoslavia and some of the Eastern-bloc nations won't be far behind. Inevitably, their rising tides of intensely competitive exports — of manufactured goods, increasingly — will generate even stronger pressures for protectionism in this country; to the extent that Congress and the President acquiesce, American productivity may suffer even further and inflation will persist.

The years ahead will be marked by dwindling supplies of easily extracted resources— minerals and especially the supply of energy. It takes no great clairvoyance to see a period of wrenching readjustment ahead for this and other industrialized nations as the adaptation to shortages — and the resulting economic dislocations — proceed; the shift from cheap to expensive energy will continue to be felt uncomfortably.

There will be further progress in energy conservation—out of necessity as much as out of conviction. And, of course, there will be further development of alternatives to oil. But it will be halting. Solar energy is many times more expensive than oil or gas — and will continue so through the Eighties; geothermal will make only a modest contribution, too. Despite the enormous resources of coal this country possesses — more than Saudi Arabia and the rest of the Persian Gulf in energy equivalent — its increased use will come slowly. It will take an enormous amount of expensive capital to develop additional mining capacity; and there will be continued opposition to such expansion on environmental grounds — pollution and the warming effect of increasing carbon dioxide.

Because of the concern for safety and the environment, there will be a lack of enthusiasm for nuclear energy. Government studies have shown that the cost of building new nuclear facilities has ballooned to the point where they won't be economical for perhaps a decade, even with government subsidies. Declining oil consumption also reduces the need to invest so much in nuclear plants. So it would be the 1990s, after a reversal in economic trends and government policies, before a significantly increased contribution from nuclear power can materialize. In the meantime, the dreary fact will remain that the U.S.—and most of the world—will continue to be dependent on imported crude.

You have to assume that oil prices will be going steadily—relentlessly—higher. Though there may be temporary periods of oversupply in world markets, the oil cartel can be counted on to keep forcing the cost of crude ever upward through its control of production. Even if there are no new disruptions like the oil embargo of 1973 or the cutbacks in Iran that began with the fall of the Shah, the foreign oil producers will adjust the balance between supply and demand to keep diverting the West's wealth to their own coffers. A study by the Congressional Budget Office projects the *lowest* price likely by 1990 at $84 a barrel. The rate of rise won't be nearly as fast as in 1974 or in 1979-80, but there would still be a cumulative increase of more than 250% if these forecasters are right.

Rising energy costs will contribute to keeping inflation a major economic problem through much—if not all—of the Eighties. Scarcities of metals and minerals will work in that direction, too. Food will stoke up those fires still further under pressure of growing world demand. The liberalized depreciation allowances voted by Congress at President Reagan's request will spur business investment in more modern and efficient capacity, but the country's troublesome productivity problems will not vanish overnight; still lagging productivity could keep labor costs rising. And the fact that incomes are still indexed for so many Americans—tied loosely or tightly to some barometer or other—will tend to reduce pressure for sustained, follow-through action to cool off inflation.

One can hope that the rise in the price indexes will begin to subside soon, but previous forecasts of deceleration over the past decade have turned out incorrect. Actually, for some years now, each succeeding business upswing has begun with the inflation rate at a higher level than at the same point in the previous cycle. The pattern could yet be repeated if short-term concerns lead to a stress on quick-fix stimulation to business activity instead of longer-lasting, less appealing, inflation-dampening approaches.

The best case you can make is for a moderate slowing in the rate of rise in the price indexes—for the next three or four years, at any rate. Conceivably, the credit-controlling Federal Reserve will be able to stick to its tough tight-money policy and succeed in curbing the growth of the money supply. And, hopefully, President Reagan's tax cuts and other Federal government actions will encourage investment leading to greater productivity and increased, price-curbing supplies. If there are no sudden calamities that send key costs rocketing, the basic over-all measures of price change could throttle back to a 6%-a-year rate of climb.

But analysts worry that everything won't go just right and permit the inflation rate to subside to this degree in the years just ahead. They feel that it is safer to assume that it will continue at a point or two below the pace at which the Eighties began—an underlying or basic rate of 9% or 10%; disruptive events could push the rate even higher for some periods. But forecasters would rule out hyperinflation—so-called South American inflation, with price indexes climbing at 30%, 50%, or even more rapidly each year.

The ups and downs of the business cycle will continue to recur. Swings could be as pronounced and destabilizing as in the Seventies. Stop-and-go efforts to combat inflation could contribute to the instability; it remains to be seen whether the Reagan Administration can evolve more consistent policies. In any case, a Great Depression—a prolonged period of high unemployment and severe decline in business activity—is not likely. If economists have learned one thing, it is how to reflate an economy—with easy money and stepped-up Federal spending—even if they haven't found out how to contain the resultant inflation. Political pressures would force even the most well-meaning administration to shift its priorities to fighting unemployment should the jobless rate approach 10%.

Interest rates will continue to fluctuate widely, especially if the credit-controlling Federal Reserve System adheres to anything like the policy it adopted in late 1979 of trying to steady the money supply's growth. Rates may not go much above the peak levels of January 1981 nor get down any time soon to the lows reached in the spring of 1980; the "Fed" may take steps to limit the most extreme destabilizing swings. But the amplitude of the movements will be large by pre-1980 standards.

The fastest-growing areas of the country will continue to be those that have led the way over the past two decades—and for the same reason: These sections will keep expanding at a healthy rate because of climate and resources. Population growth will continue to stagnate in the old industrial sections of the Mid-West and New England, though the latter will see some revitalization from its high-technology enterprises. But the migration to the Southeast, the West, and the Southwest will continue though at a less rapid pace. Specifically, the big-growth states will be Florida, Texas, New Mexico, Arizona, California, Colorado, and Wyoming. To zero in more precisely, the big-growth cities will be Albuquerque, Anaheim, Austin, Baton Rouge, Dallas, Denver, El Paso, Houston, Las Vegas, Memphis, Miami, Portland (Ore.), Phoenix, San Jose, Salt Lake City, Tampa, and Tucson. There will be further rehabilitation of the centers of some large cities, and some population inflow, but it will be overshadowed by the continued development of the suburbs for both living and industry.

The U.S. economy will continue to shift away from its emphasis on heavy industry—steel, autos, nonferrous mining—at perhaps an accelerated rate. The stress will increasingly be on high technology—genetic engineering, electronics, plastics, other synthetics that will replace metals, and data processing. The use of personal computers will be extended to the home; videodisks will open a new vista for consumer electronics.

No big rise in the standard of living seems

likely, at least in the early Eighties. Despite the Reagan tax cuts, individuals will still be hard put to keep incomes ahead of inflation. The trend to two-income families will continue, but at a measurably slower rate now that the percentage of women in the labor force has moved up so substantially. Corporate profits may continue to rise, but—after realistic adjustments for the cost of replacing worn-out plant and equipment—will actually lag for many companies and industries.

The U.S. population will keep aging. There will be fewer persons in the twenty-three-to-thirty-four-year-old age group and more in the older ranges. The number of retirees seeking the sun and able to support themselves will grow. The ratio of those paying Social Security taxes to those drawing benefits will continue to fall, putting the system under increasing fiscal pressure.

The demand for housing will be strong in the Eighties as the members of the postwar baby generation reach home-buying age. The trend to single-person households and the obsolescence of older units will add to the demand. Some analysts see brisker building activity than in the Seventies—certainly more than 1½ million new homes a year in the immediate future and nearly 2½ million by 1989. But the typical home will tend to be smaller, less elaborate, featuring new fuel-efficient designs and new materials—more town houses and condominiums and fewer detached, single-family units. The cost of maintaining a home will rise substantially—relative to income as well as absolutely. And higher mortgage rates are here to stay, now that Congress and government agencies have acted to give savers higher returns on their money. Finally, after the slight hesitation as the Eighties began, home prices could again rise as fast—or even faster—than the Consumer Price Index. A home will remain one of the best inflation hedges for many families.

To sum up, the Eighties aren't shaping up as anything like an idyllic era—a period of happier days and diminishing problems. But the world won't be coming to an end, either. It will still be possible for the alert investor to increase his wealth and well-being—even after allowing for the inroads of inflation.

The foregoing chapters were necessary to provide a springboard, a framework, for talking in detail about the investments you should—or should not—be going into if you want to make as much money as you can with the least amount of risk. Now come discussions of specific possibilities, starting with a large and important group—the fixed-income securities.

SECTION II

INCOME (AND SAFETY) FIRST

CHAPTER FIVE

LIFE INSURANCE BEFORE ALL ELSE

FAIL-SAFE RATING ON . . .

Safety: The savings portions of whole life premiums are invested in quality instruments by insurers under state supervision and therefore generally rank as safe as, say, corporate bonds.

Income: The rates of interest on these savings are relatively low.

Tax status: Generally, death benefits are untaxed but earnings on savings withdrawn before death are taxed as ordinary income.

The point is made in Chapter Three that life insurance has a role to play in almost every investment plan. The younger the family, the more the protection that's needed. And it should be arranged for before any money is put into stocks or bonds or any other investment.

But life insurance can be more than just a family's protection against financial disaster. It can also be an investment. In one major form of insurance, part of the premium accumulates as interest-earning savings. Is this form a good buy? If not, what are the alternatives?

Life insurance is a complex subject. Most people find it so formidable that they turn off, leaving the choice of the right kinds and the amounts of coverage to agents, each of whom usually represents one or more companies with specific products to push. There's a lot of truth to the old cliché that says life insurance isn't bought—it's sold!

But you shouldn't let the choice of what kind and how much pass to others by default. You can and should make the decisions yourself. To begin with, here is a way you can determine the amount of protection you should have:

- **Calculate how much the family survivors will need** to live on each year, once the insured passes on. (Say, $20,000.)
- **Multiply that by the number of years** until the youngest child is on his or her own and the spouse can get a job if not already employed. Her income can be deducted from the annual need. (We'll use nine years in this example.)
- **Reckon in the costs of college** for all your children. (Two kids at $40,000 each.)
- **Then deduct the Social Security benefits** that the family can collect until the youngest child is eighteen—or older, if he or she stays in school. (Nine years times $7,000.)
- **Don't forget to figure in the proceeds**

from any group insurance policy that may cover you as part of the fringe benefits provided by an employer. (Assume $25,000.)

In this example, we would come up with a need for about $172,000, without allowing for any income that a widow would earn. We can't ignore the impact of inflation, which could increase the total needed, but the income from investing the insurance proceeds would go a long way toward offsetting the erosion—for several years, at any rate.

Now—what kind of insurance? Essentially, there are two basic types:

Ordinary Life—or whole life or straight life—builds up a cash value over the life of the policy in addition to providing a stated amount of benefits to survivors on the death of the insured. That money can be cashed in on termination of the policy, and it can be borrowed against at relatively low rates—about 8% on a new policy at major companies. The cash position, which accumulates slowly over the first five to ten years, grows more rapidly thereafter. And it earns interest, year by year. What's more, the premium set at the outset can remain level for the life of the policy—meaning no big jumps as the years roll on.

Term Insurance is the other major category of life insurance. It provides protection only; there is no element of savings in the premium paid. If premium payments cease, there is no accumulation of money to cash in. And policy-holders cannot borrow on this insurance. Premiums per $1,000 of insurance rise, usually every five years, as the insured grows older.

Proponents of ordinary life insurance say that it is often the only way that a family head who is not a good financial manager can discipline himself to save. But, realistically, term insurance seems to offer more—especially to the younger person who needs all the protection he or she can get, but whose means of paying for it are limited.

Term-insurance premiums are lower—often as

little as a third of the cost of a standard ordinary-life policy for a man aged thirty-five. The amount of built-in commissions to agents is less, too—relatively as well as absolutely.

Inflation erodes the value of the savings accumulating in a whole-life policy. At current rates of depreciation in the dollar's purchasing power, the $50,000 building up as part of a nest egg would be worth less than a third twenty years hence. (So, of course, would the principal value of a twenty-year bond.) But with term insurance you pay for only the current year's protection.

The bottom line in most cases is the interest rate that life-insurance companies pay on the savings that accumulate in a whole-life policy compared with what is available on alternative places to put your money. These days, insurance companies would pay as much as 9% or more, depending on the earnings of their investments, their loss experience, and other factors, over the life of a new policy.

But in periods of high inflation—and that's what prudence suggests to expect for a long time to come—other investments offer more. You would be better off buying a term policy and putting the savings in premiums into one of those alternatives.

Whatever kind of insurance you decide to buy, it will pay to shop around—the way you would for a car, furniture, or a TV set. The costs of roughly similar policies can vary as much as 30% or more for the same amount of insurance. Look up agents from several different companies in the Yellow Pages, tell them what and how much you want, and ask for the best prices they can give you. Tell them that you are shopping around.

Go slow in buying life insurance through the mail. There doesn't have to be anything wrong with it; the policies some companies offer may be cheaper because their selling costs are lower. What's more, mail-order buying is convenient. But you may be limited in the amount you can buy, and some companies—to avoid the need for a medical examination—pay only partial benefits in, say, the first two years after a policy is bought.

There is still one other investment aspect of life insurance that's worth discussing at this point: What to do with the benefits when the insured dies or when the policyholder just decides to terminate the policy? Here are some possibilities that beneficiaries can refer to; they are not tremendously attractive on the whole:

• *Taking the money in a lump sum*—if the beneficiary is good at managing money or could employ the services of someone who is. Otherwise consider . . .

• *Leaving the funds with the insurance company*, taking out only the interest earned at, say, quarterly intervals. (Note, though, that insurers don't pay much if any more than savings banks in this connection.) Sometimes it's wise to choose this option for, say, a year, using the time to make careful alternative arrangements. But if the interest payments aren't large enough to meet needs, consider . . .

• *Choosing a fixed-period option* under which the beneficiary receives the interest plus installment payments of the principal over a set number of years—ten years, fifteen years, or, say, however long it takes to see kids through college.

• *Alternatively, consider receiving a fixed amount of benefits* until the entire amount specified in the policy has been paid out.

• *And, finally, there is the option of converting* the benefits into an annuity as a source of income over a fixed period of years—or for the remaining life of the beneficiary. Because of the low interest rate earned by the money, this is not an attractive alternative.

Note: Earnings on many of these options enjoy a $1,000 interest exclusion from income taxes each year.

CHAPTER SIX

SAVINGS FOR A RAINY DAY

FAIL-SAFE RATING ON . . .

Safety: Federal insurance makes covered deposits as good as Treasury securities. Amounts above coverage level are quite safe, as well, because of the government supervision given banks and savings institutions.

Income: In one case, yields offered approach the highest available, but most do not.

Tax Status: Fully taxable at the Federal, state, and local levels—except for retirement-type accounts, which are really "tax deferred." Since January 1, 1981, and continuing for at least two years, $200 in interest and dividends has been deductible per taxpayer—$400 for a married couple.

After you have arranged for adequate insurance, there is one other pre-investment precaution that you should take — setting up a savings account at a bank or a thrift institution. It's true that so-called passbook savings — the kind you can withdraw at a moment's notice — earn what seems like a pittance in this era of very high interest rates, even though government regulators are in the process of removing the long-standing restriction on paying more, which will mean changes in some of the features of the investments described below and perhaps some brand-new types as well. But it is important to set up a ready source of funds that can be tapped quickly in an emergency, even if it's only a bare minimum — enough for your family to get by on for a month or two. The rate of return may have to be a secondary consideration.

> To be sure, there are alternative liquid investments such as money-market mutual funds, Treasury bills, and others that can be cashed in very quickly if necessary. But, as we'll show in later chapters, they might involve a loss if, say, a Treasury bill is sold in a declining market before it matures. And as we'll see when they are discussed in Chapter Twelve, yields on money-market funds could go down at some point, reducing their advantage significantly.

Anyway, it's a good idea to have an established relationship with a bank or savings and loan association—something more than keeping a checking account. This is especially true if you think you might need to borrow some money in the foreseeable future to purchase a home, make an investment, or any other reason; a customer has a better chance of getting a loan when money is tight.

One way to make up for some of the loss of interest that you will suffer by putting cash into a deposit account instead of a high-yielding investment is to start earning interest on your checking account by opening a NOW account at a bank or savings institution. Since January 1, 1981, they have been allowed to pay interest on what are really checking accounts. So you can earn 5¼% on what were formerly non-interest-bearing checking deposits at banks, savings banks, and savings and loans, which couldn't offer such service in most states until recently.

There are some strings attached, though, and they could offset the value of NOW accounts to you. You'll have to keep a balance of as little as $50 in some cases or as much as $3,000 at the other extreme; if you go below—even for a day—you may be hit for service charges that could typically range from $2 to $5 per month. And you may have to pay fees of, say, 14 cents or 15 cents for each check you write in excess of an allowable number, plus 8 cents or 10 cents for each deposit you make. You could, conceivably, end up paying more in charges than you earn in interest. So check a few places and calculate the advantages and disadvantages of any particular plan in the light of the number of checks you write and what you might earn on money you invest elsewhere.

Banks and thrift institutions still have authority to issue non-negotiable certificates of deposit in minimum denominations of as little as $100 at interest rates varying with the maturity from 5½% for a ninety-day CD (at a commercial bank) to 8% for an eight-year CD (at a savings and loan). And, not too long ago, a new shorter-term, higher-yielding CD was added to the list (see below).

One advantage these CD's—and the more popular flexible-rate types we'll talk about below—offer is the fact that, like any other bank deposits, they are insured by the Federal government in amounts up to $100,000 per account. Moreover, you can borrow up to 90% of the face value of these certificates at an interest rate varying from 2 to 5 percentage points above that of the CD itself. Finally, unlike market investments, the value of these CD's does not fluctuate. Any time you cash them in you will receive the full face value, plus accrued interest—less any penalty that might be imposed for premature withdrawals.

There are two large disadvantages to such CD's, though. First, their yields can be measurably below market yields obtainable elsewhere when money is tight. Second, the penalties for early withdrawal can be stiff. So, once you buy one of these certificates, you may be locked in. If you cash them in before they mature you suffer a large loss of interest. (See below)

The money-market certificate has been a highly popular investment at banks and savings and loans. It is a certificate of deposit which matures in six months and is sold in minimums of $10,000. The formula that determines the rate of interest paid is set by Federal regulatory officials at their discretion and so is subject to change; it is basically related to the discount rate of interest on the Treasury's six-month bill. Interest cannot be compounded.

There is a way around the $10,000 minimum requirement—"loophole" CD's. The bank or savings institutions will lend you, say, $5,000, keeping the CD as security for the loan. You pay 1 or 2 percentage points over the rate you get on the amount borrowed.

At the start of 1981, this was how rates on money-market certificates could vary under the then prevailing formula.

When the Treasury bill rate is	The top rate a commercial bank can pay is	And the top rate a thrift institution can pay is
8.75% and above	Bill rate plus .25%	Bill rate plus .25%
8.5% to 8.75%	Bill rate plus .25%	9.0%
7.5% to 8.5%	Bill rate plus .25%	Bill rate plus .50%
7.25% to 7.5%	7.75%	Bill rate plus .50%
Below 7.25%	7.75%	7.75%

The rules can also change for the two-and-a-half-year certificate designed primarily to give so-called small savers the opportunity to earn interest rates close to those available on marketable securities.

Early in 1981, savings banks and savings and loans could pay as much as comparable 2½-year Treasury securities— up to a maximum of 12%. Commercial banks can pay a quarter-point less. Even when the rate on the Treasuries is below 9%, though, savings banks and savings and loans can continue to offer up to 9½%, commercial banks up to 9¼%, under the formula set by the authorities in mid-1980 (but subject to modification at any time). The Treasury posts a new benchmark rate for these CD's—based on the market yields of its notes of comparable maturity—every two weeks. Daily compounding is permitted and can sweeten the yield.

Though there is no minimum amount required by the regulatory authorities for the 2½-year CD's, banks and S&L's began by requiring $500 to $1,000 minimum investments. The rates offered could at times be somewhat more or less than those available from money-market mutual funds—and the deposits are not liquid, unless you are willing to pay a penalty for premature withdrawal. But the certificates are convenient to buy and the minimum denominations are smaller than the amounts required on six-month money-market certificates as well as those of money-market mutual funds. If short-term rates decline, the new certificates could conceivably be yielding more than the mutual funds or the six-month certificates.

Penalties for early cash-in of these CD's are stiff. Savers would be hit for loss of the interest earned if they turn in a CD with less than three months' original maturity. They would lose three months of interest on the amount of funds withdrawn from a CD of original maturity of three months to one year, regardless of how much interest was actually earned; indeed, if less than three months' worth was earned, the deposit being returned would be less than was originally invested. On CD's with original maturities of more than a year, there is a loss of interest on the amount withdrawn equal to what would have been earned in six months.

A word about deposit insurance: Both the Federal Deposit Insurance Corp. and the Federal Savings and Loan Insurance Corp. insure each account up to $100,000. But a husband and wife could have as many as five separate accounts (as individuals, each as trustee for the other, and jointly). Each of those would be insured up to $100,000. If there are children, even more combinations are possible.

CHAPTER SEVEN

THE WHY AND HOW
OF FIXED-INCOME SECURITIES

Many financial experts believe that the once gilt-edged sheen of bonds and other fixed-income securities has been irreparably tarnished. Inflation has made them poor—no, disastrous—investments. They should henceforth be avoided like the plague.

Unfortunately, there is a lot of truth in that sweeping indictment. Those who bought bonds and other long-term issues during the Seventies and before have found themselves holding securities that pay what must now be viewed as pitifully low interest rates. What's more, the market prices of these assets have been pounded down—in quite a few cases to 70 cents on the dollar or less; anyone who has had to sell out in the past year or two has suffered a relatively large loss on his money. That's not what was supposed to happen to bonds, once considered the safest investments of them all.

The trouble is that, all too often, even long-term fixed-income securities paying current rates no longer yield a decent rate of return. Inflation has been proceeding at rates close to—and at times even higher than—the rates bonds and similar issues pay.

When the taxes paid on the interest are reckoned in, the investor may end up actually losing money. If he isn't, he is no doubt very close to doing so.

Fortunately, the same problem does not afflict short-term interest-earning securities— so-called money-market instruments, which we'll talk about in Chapter Twelve. When money is tight, they offer more than long-terms. And they come due after only three or six months or, say, a year. This means that the investor can get his money back and then put it into a higher-yielding asset fairly quickly; he doesn't have to suffer lower-than-prevailing rates for very long. And he wouldn't have to take a substantial loss if he had to sell out before his securities' maturity; market prices of short-term issues don't fluctuate nearly as widely as long-terms.

But don't write off long-term fixed-income securities entirely. They may still have a place in an investment program—for example, where it is imperative to be assured of a dependable number of dollars coming in to support a retirement income. What's more, when bonds are purchased at the right time—at or near the peak of an interest-rate surge—they can be good buys. As interest rates fall back, the yields on the bonds can exceed the rate of inflation by a comfortable margin. And, instead of taking a loss on sale before maturity, the investor could come out with a profit.

The reason why will become clear later on. Now, though, let's talk about some common characteristics of all fixed-income securities—what, precisely, they are . . . the various interest-rate concepts and how they differ . . . and how the bond and money markets work.

A FEW DEFINITIONS

You no doubt already have a very clear idea of what constitutes a fixed-income obligation. But, just to be thorough, let's review a few definitions.

A fixed-income security is a legal contract between a borrower—government or private—and a lender . . . in this case, you. The security presents a legally binding promise on the part of the issuer to pay you a fixed amount of interest, usually twice a year, and repay the principal or face amount of the security at a specified time. These debt instruments are usually but not always negotiable—that is, resellable to others.

But there are variations among fixed-income securities. Some, for example, carry explicit or implicit Federal government guarantees, some are backed by the full faith and credit of a state government. Some are, in effect, well secured by specific items of property, like a home; others are little more than IOU's. These differences, along with the solidity of the issuer, normally are reflected in the rates that each type of security pays. The safest, most secure, pay the lowest rates, and the most speculative pay the highest.

Fixed-income securities also vary by maturity—the period of time between their issuance and the date they come due for payoff. Obligations put out for a year or less are termed short-term securities. Those with due dates between one and five or ten years are said to be intermediates and could be called longer-term. Issues sold for as long as twenty or thirty years or longer are the real long-term maturities.

These definitions exclude common stocks, even those which have paid dividends regularly for years. If you own a common stock, you own a piece of the corporation. But if you own a bond or similar debt instrument, you are a creditor of that corporation; you get your interest payments before the stockholders get their dividend checks.

Preferred stock resembles a fixed-income security, even though it really is not one. It is more of a hybrid, reflecting characteristics of both a share of stock and a bond. It carries a fixed payment rate like a bond, and its price is affected by movements in interest rates generally. But, while preferreds are entitled to dividends before commons, the bondholders get paid before owners of preferred stock.

If you were to rank debt securities in order of safety, you would put U.S. Treasury bonds, notes, and bills at the head of the line, followed quickly by Federal government agencies; then would come the notes and bonds issued by state and local governments or their sponsored agencies; next, you'd put the securities issued in the U.S. by some foreign governments and international institutions such as the World Bank; finally would come the variety of bonds, notes, and other securities issued by corporations and a range of financial institutions. Of course, there are variations in "quality" within each category; thus, some corporate securities are safer than some state and local government issues, and so on. But in general that is the way the market would tend to rank the safety—or, conversely, the risk—of these issues.

PRINCIPLES OF INTEREST

In all the chapters of this section, and in some others as well, we will be talking about the interest rates and yields carried by various types of investments. But it might be helpful, before we do that, to define precisely what they are and how they are figured. Some of what follows is quite simple; you probably know it already. But the discussion will be useful in examining some complex and technical points later on. Some readers may be a little confused by the formulas and numbers we will occasionally be using here. Don't be. Most of them are used just to illustrate a point. We will walk you through these calculations step by step, explaining as we go along. Our primary intent is to explain concepts and then show you how you can use them if you want to do some figuring for yourself.

First, let's define what we mean by interest. Interest is simply the price someone pays for the use—or hire—of someone else's money. When it comes to investments, it is almost always expressed as an annual rate. If the stated interest rate on a bond is 10%, that means the borrower pays 10% of the face value of the bond to the bondholder every year. If it is a $1,000 bond (and most bonds are sold in units of $1,000) the borrower pays the holder $100 annually.

There are two basic methods of computing interest that you will run across most often—simple and compound.

Simple interest is interest paid periodically as just described above. It is the kind most often used by issuers of bonds and notes such as the U.S. Treasury or corporations. To repeat, though: Simple interest is expressed as an annual rate. If a borrower promises to pay 10% on a $1,000 note issued for only six months, you will not receive $100. You will get only $50. If the note matures in three months you get $25—and so on. It's like the concept of speed when you are driving; if you are going at 60 miles an hour, but travel for only a half hour, you cover only thirty miles.

Compound interest is the kind most banks and savings institutions pay on your savings accounts and sometimes on certificates of deposit. Similarly, investment plans which reinvest your dividends or earnings are, in effect, offering you a form of compound interest. Compounding simply means adding interest earned in one period to your original deposit or investment and then, in the following period, calculating future interest payments on that new, higher figure.

Let's say that your bank offers to pay you 5% interest on your savings compounded annually. At the end of one year you have earned $50. That is added to your original $1,000 deposit. If you allow that money to remain in your savings account for another year, not only does your original $1,000 earn interest but the $50 the bank added at the end of the first year also earns 5% interest. So instead of earning only $50 in interest during the second year you earn $52.50 ($1,050 x 5%) and have $1,102.50 at the end of two years.

Usually, a bank will compound your money more often than once a year. It might advertise compounding quarterly, monthly, or even daily. The important thing to remember is that when compounding is done less often than once a year the bank adds a smaller amount to your account each time it compounds, but it does so more often. For example, if it offers 5% compounded quarterly, that means that at the end of each three months an amount equal to 1.25% (5% divided by 4) of the amount in your account is added to your constantly growing principal. The more frequent the compounding the better off you are.

To see how this works out in practice, and what it means to you, let's examine two hypothetical accounts. Each is for $1,000, and each is opened on January 1. The first pays 5% compounded annually, the other 5% compounded quarterly. Account number one pays you the $50 at the end of the year, bringing your balance to $1,050; at the end of the second year, as noted above, you will end up with $1,102.50 in the first account. But with account number two, interest is paid and credited to your account each quarter beginning on March 31. On that date the bank pays you 1.25% interest, or $12.50, bringing you up to $1,012.50. Then, on June 30, the bank pays you another 1.25% but this time it pays interest not on $1,000 but on your new balance, $1,012.50 The interest amounts to $12.66, bringing your total to $1,025.16. The same thing happens at the end of the third quarter and again at the end of the fourth. By that time you have accumulated, not $50 in interest, but $50.95—and you have $1,050.95 in your account. So, while the bank is paying you 5%, compounding brings the yield—the equivalent simple-interest rate—to nearly 5.1%; and at the end of the second year, you will have $1,104.49 in the second account, $1.99 more than in the first one.

Obviously, it is possible for the bank to carry this compounding idea to any extreme. It costs banks very little more to offer you daily compounding. With daily compounding, the banks would be adding only slightly more than one hundredth of one percent to your account daily (nearly 0.14% to be precise). That would result in an annual yield to you of 5.13%.

Now we come to the distinction between an interest rate and a yield, a distinction that confuses many, but which means a lot to the investor. The easiest way to keep the two concepts straight is to keep in mind that the yield is what you receive while the interest rate is what the borrower pays. Sometimes the two are the same, but often they are not. We've already seen how the compounding of interest affects the return to you on a savings deposit; your yield of 5.1% is higher than the 5% rate the bank has formally written into your passbook. Let's now look at another example, one you will frequently encounter when investing in fixed-income securities.

> Let's say you buy a corporate bond bearing a 10% interest rate. You pay exactly the face amount, $1,000. The corporation sends you an interest payment of $100. (Actually it is usually $50, twice a year.) In this case, the interest rate the corporation pays and the yield you receive are exactly the same: 10%.

But suppose you bought the bond from someone else and did not pay its face value. (We'll go into how this could happen later.) Suppose you paid $990 for the $1,000 bond. The corporation will still send a check for $50 twice a year, so the interest rate it keeps paying out on its indebtedness to you twice each year remains 10%. But, because you paid less than the face value, the yield is more than 10%; it is, in this case, 10.1%.

That is called the current yield. To figure out the current yield of any bond all you have to do is divide the annual interest payment by the actual price you paid for the bond. In this case: $100 divided by $990=0.101 dollars for each dollar of the bond's face value—or an interest rate of 10.1%.

Since you almost never deal in figures that are so conveniently neat and round, let's take another, more realistic example. Let's say you buy a bond that pays 9⅝% interest and you pay a price of $970.65. To find the current yield — the simple return on your money — you divide the interest you receive ($96.25 per $1,000) by the price you paid ($970.65) and get 9.92%. (Yes — it does help to have a small pocket calculator.)

We've talked a lot about the current yield. But there is yet another yield concept to deal with, one which many investors regard as far more important than current yield. **This is the idea of yield to maturity.** This is the yield figure you most often see quoted in newspaper bond tables. In essence, this concept takes into account not only how much current interest you may earn on the bond but also any built-in capital gain or loss you will take if you hold a bond purchased above or below its issue price until it comes due.

Often, you will not pay face value for bonds you buy whether you purchase them when they are originally issued or afterward in what is known as the secondary or resale market. You may pay a little more or a little less on a new issue. That's because the original issue price may have been set by competitive bidding among dealers and investors who will calculate their bids to several decimal places in order to get the securities for the lowest price and as close to the going market as possible. The issuer usually sets the rate it pays to the nearest higher ⅛-point fraction, so that the price to the buyer is less than par — that is, 100. The price to you or any other later buyer can also be affected by market developments over time, which can produce a big change in the bond's market price.

Let's say you buy a bond that has a face value of $1,000 for $900. And let's further assume there are two years left until the bond is set to come due. If the bond is paying 7½% interest ($75.00 a year), the current yield is 8.33%. ($75 divided by $900). But if you hold this bond to maturity, you will also realize a profit of $100 on the day it is redeemed by the issuing corporation, because the company promised to pay $1,000 even though you only paid $900.

So the total return to you includes not only the interest paid over the years by the bond but also the capital gain you realize when you cash it in. That gain has to be taken into account when you calculate the true yield of this security. The mathematical formula for doing so precisely is complex. But there is a quick way to figure an approximate yield to maturity that is adequate in most cases.

You are going to earn a $100 capital gain on this security in two years. So, in accounting for the $100, you add $50 a year ($100 divided by two years = $50) to the $75 annual yield you receive to arrive at an adjusted interest figure of $125. The price of the bond will fluctuate over the years as interest rates rise and fall but will gradually approach its face value as it nears its maturity date, when it will be worth exactly $1,000. You must take that final price into account to calculate the average price, you do this by adding the redemption price ($1,000) and the price you paid ($900) then dividing by two to get $950. You then divide the adjusted interest ($125) by the average price ($950) and you get 13.2%. That is your yield to maturity, within about two tenths of a percentage point.

This is the most-often quoted yield and the one that is easiest to get from your newspaper or broker. You will almost never have to make this calculation yourself in deciding to buy a bond. The above discussion, though, still does not take into account several other factors which will affect the net return to you, including brokers, fees and tax considerations. These will be discussed later on.

One more form of paying interest is dis-

counting, which you run into in buying certain types of Treasury securities—Treasury bills, specifically. In selling bills, the Treasury actually offers them at a discount from the face value it will repay at maturity. The difference between the original selling price and the face value represents the interest you earn.

Incidentally, the "bill rate" that is most often referred to in reporting on what is happening to Treasury bills is the so-called discount rate. It is computed on a 360-day year by dividing the face amount of the bill into the interest paid. (See the chapter that follows for an illustration of how the discount rate is calculated.)

Let's step back now and take a look at how the market for these securities is organized and functions. For this discussion, for the sake of brevity, we'll use the term bond to mean all types of fixed-income securities unless the different periods for which bonds or notes or bills are issued are themselves significant in the illustration.

THE BOND AND MONEY MARKETS

The bond and money markets are where all those fixed-income issues we will be talking about are bought and sold. They aren't found in centralized locations, like the stock exchanges, though some bonds are listed on the exchanges. Rather, the great bulk of fixed-income securities are traded through an informal network made up of specialized dealers and major brokerage houses. In recent years, as much as $150 billion in new securities of this type have been issued annually. In any one day, these dealers buy and sell billions of dollars, worth of corporate and government securities— some for their own accounts, some for customers. Most of their customers are large institutions—banks, insurance companies, or pension funds. The daily dollar volume usually exceeds that done in stocks. Most trades are made over the telephone. Large profits or losses may be recorded daily in brokers' or dealers' ledgers.

And this brings up a critically important point only brief-

ly alluded to so far but which must be remembered in dealing with all fixed-income securities.

*Their market prices can vary, sometimes
sharply,* day to day, with prevailing financial conditions.
To be sure, the annual interest payments are fixed, along
with the amount of principal you'll get back at maturity.
But, in the interval before a security becomes due, its price
can move up . . . and it can come down. That's academic,
of course, if you simply plan to hold the bond to maturity.
But suppose you want to turn it into cash, or you have to,
before maturity?

On one memorable day not too long ago, a large group of
underwriters—syndicates of financial firms whose business
is to buy up whole issues and distribute them to investors—
lost a staggering $50 million because of the price drop in a
single issue: new bonds being sold by IBM—the International Business Machines Corporation. Ironically, the syndicate included some of the biggest names on Wall Street and
the company was and is regarded as one of the safest, most
secure corporate issuers in the world. The underwriters, all
savvy market pros, took one of the worst financial drub-
bings in history. So, in fact, did any individual or institution
which bought IBM's bonds on the day they were offered
and had to sell them not too long after.

What happened? Why did all these knowledgeable
people drop so much money? Did they get stuck with a bad
security?

To answer the last question first: No—they did not. In
fact, it was precisely because IBM is such a good security
that so many people took such a bath. Underwriters jumped
at the chance to take part in a historic rare debt offering of
the world's leading computer company. But, because the
market went sour, they had to sell to avoid risking even
greater losses; they operate with a lot of borrowed money,
bearing heavy interest costs, and can't afford to hold for
very long bonds whose prices could, conceivably, go even
lower. For most of those underwriters, there is no way they
can recoup the losses, once they have sold out below the

price they paid. Their money is just gone. The investors who bought IBM's bonds from the underwriters also took a loss — at least, temporarily, on paper — of about $90 for each $1,000 they invested.

The important thing to remember is that the loss was only on paper for investors who didn't sell out. It will only become an actual loss if they decide to get out at a depressed level. Some will, for tax purposes; others may do so just because they need the cash. But many will hold on to the bonds and continue to collect the $93.75 in interest the bond pays annually for each $1,000 unit. They will watch the value of their investment rise and fall over the years until they, or their heirs, cash the bonds in at maturity for full face value.

So we come to a lesson that every investor must learn before entering this or any other market:

There are very few absolutely safe investments. That's true no matter what you buy — even securities issued by the U.S. government, which will never default or fail to pay interest. You run the risk of a loss if you must sell out at an inopportune time.

That risk is called "market risk." The term simply means that, because of very broad movements in interest rates, the market price of even the safest fixed-income securities will fluctuate. There is no way around that fact of investment life.

Back to the case of IBM. On the day the price on its bonds was set, yields of roughly comparable issues were in the neighborhood of 9.4% to 9.6%. But, shortly thereafter, the Federal Reserve Board announced a new policy which had the effect of driving all interest rates sharply higher very quickly — before all the IBM bonds could be sold. With higher yields available in the market, no sensible investor would any longer consider the IBM's — not unless the price was cut enough to bring the yield on the IBM's up to the new market levels. Which brings up another basic fact of fixed-income securities life that many find difficult to grasp:

When yields on marketable securities go up, the prices of such securities go down. And the reverse, of course, is also true.

IBM gave a dramatic example of how interest-rate fluctuations can affect the prices of fixed-income securities. Usually the sort of fluctuations that hit IBM do not happen that quickly. But more modest movements do occur all the time. These days, interest rates are constantly on the move. They are much more volatile, as a by-product of the strategy the credit-controlling Federal Reserve System has been pursuing since October 1979 to control the nation's money supply—and, hence, inflation. The Fed aims at providing the banking system with a steady, though moderate stream of new lending power. In essence, when this supply falls short of (or exceeds) the demand for money, interest rates are free to rise (or fall)—and they do so, often abruptly.

But, if you plan to invest for the long term—that is, buy a bond and hold it for the income it produces—you won't be directly affected when its market value rises and falls, with fluctuations in the business cycle.

Normally, when the economy is expanding, interest rates move up, in response to rising demands for money and efforts by the Federal Reserve to fight inflation; the prices of already outstanding bonds fall correspondingly. Eventually, the business expansion peaks out and a recession sets in. When that happens, interest rates usually come down, sometimes quickly, sometimes slowly, and bond prices rise again.

As noted earlier, moves in short-term rates—those on securities that mature in a year or less—are more volatile than long-term; they move up or down more rapidly in any given period—up faster when money is getting tighter, down faster when it is getting easier to come by. One reason for the difference: When money is tight, borrowers are willing to pay extra because they won't be doing so for long and the absolute number of dollars they pay won't be so large; but they would think carefully about committing themselves to pay high rates for ten, twenty, or thirty years.

In normal times, defined as those in which inflation is relatively moderate, short-term interest rates tend to be lower than long. (Lenders want to be compensated more for tying up their money for long periods, during which they may see a step-up in inflation that would erode the value of their money.) The so-called yield curve—a chart line that shows going interest-rate levels for similar securities of successively longer maturity—slopes upward as the number of years in the scale gets longer. But the curve becomes inverted—and slopes downward—when money is scarce and short-term rates have zoomed.

For the most part, the prices of U.S. Treasury issues are only affected by such broad interest-rate movements, which in turn are affected by business trends and inflation. Except on occasions when available issues might be in short supply, perhaps because turmoil in other markets or other countries generates a "flight to quality," there are few other factors to weigh. The same is generally true of the very highest investment-grade corporate issues, such as IBM or AT&T, as well as highly rated state and local government issues.

It is safe to say that, while no one really anticipated the dramatic jump in interest rates that started in October 1979, there were probably a number of investors who bought IBM bonds even though they realized that their market value might drop some in the short run. These people may have expected interest rates to move a little higher than they were before finally peaking and turning downward again. ***But, wisely, they didn't think they could catch the very peak in rates.*** Rather than risk losing the chance to buy IBM or another issue of comparable quality at an attractive yield, they decided to commit some long-term funds. Many no doubt also expected rates to fall fairly sharply after the peaking, making their IBM's look like a bargain. If rates did fall, they would end up with a secure, quality bond, paying a higher rate of interest than new issues would offer. In effect, then, they chose to do their bond buying when the peaks in yields seemed near, with no certain knowledge that they had actually arrived. Had they had even more money to commit, a program of gradual investment at successively higher yields would have been warranted.

This may turn out to be the most sensible strategy most of the time because one of the most difficult things to do—for professional or lay investors—is to pinpoint interest-rate peaks and troughs precisely. (If you can do it, you don't have to read this book.) Most professionals, including those who manage billions of dollars of other people's money, are quite happy to buy the long-term bonds they want somewhere near the peak of the interest rate cycle. But it usually takes experience, a reliable flow of timely information, and of course, a large amount of spare time to play that game independently.

Historically, the "real" rate of interest—one that assumes no inflation at all—has always been thought to be about 3%. Many analysts add this to the inflation rate—and allow a little extra for today's high tax rates—to get what they feel is an acceptable long-term yield. Thus, if the inflation rate is 10%, a high-quality bond should yield a little more than 13%, while one that is of lower quality (see the discussions on quality ratings in Chapters Ten and Eleven) should return even more because of the greater risk.

Thus, the rate of inflation is really the key to determining whether a bond or note yield is "good" or one that is worth avoiding. And, if you have a feel about whether inflation will get better or worse, you will have a fairly good fix as to the future course of interest rates. To say, for example, that a 12% yield is high, without assessing the rate of inflation, is to run the risk of misleading yourself as to what return you are really getting on an investment. Economists call this "the money illusion." If the Republican Administration that came into office early in 1981 can successfully reduce the rate of inflation, even a little, the bond-yield highs of 1981 will be very much worth owning, indeed.

To repeat the point made early in this chapter, this doesn't mean that individual investors should avoid all long-term, fixed-income securities. To be sure, they ought to shun them when interest rates are rising on a sustained trend; that way, they won't find themselves left behind with lower yields. In such periods, there are plenty of places to park money for the short-term, as we'll see in some of the chapters that follow. When rates are in a turning-point range, though, that's the time to "extend maturity" — to lock up those high yields before rates go lower.

These days, unless you are convinced that the inflation rate is about to begin a dramatic and permanent decline, it doesn't pay to go out too far—to thirty years, for example. Many investors find two to three years a comfortable maturity — ten years at the outside. They aren't locked in for what seems to be forever, if yields suddenly spurt. And if the business cycle should show a classical postwar pattern, a two-to-three-year security could be coming due, with the funds available for reinvestment, just about when new interest rate peaks are being reached again.

How can you spot the turning ranges? That's not an easy question to answer. As noted above, you probably won't be able to hit the bull's-eye. But you can track some of the key indicators that the professionals watch.

• *One is the money supply,* which is defined in various ways. When it is growing strongly, it's a good bet that interest rates will soon be heading higher; conversely, when it remains weak for an extended period, one can feel satisfied in concluding that rates can slip some. The movements of the most important money measures are reported regularly by major newspapers. The money supply is a notoriously erratic and volatile series of numbers, but many analysts try to plot its underlying trend. Their conclusions are also reported in, say, *The Wall Street Journal* and *The New York Times*. Reading their daily bond columns can give you a feel as to what the professionals are thinking.

Again—you won't be able to pick the absolute peaks any more than they can, except by sheer dumb luck—but you should be able to come close enough, so that you can get the assured income you need without feeling that you made a big mistake.

• **_The fundamental forces at work in the economy can also provide clues to the direction of interest rates._** A solid business upturn suggests growing demand for money—and an upward tilt to rates. A high rate of inflation points that way, too. Again, the press can be a valuable source.

The country's leading papers also provide daily prices and yields for the most widely held and traded fixed-income securities.

Let's begin now to examine in some detail the various kinds of fixed-income investments available to those who are seeking maximum safety with the highest return.

CHAPTER EIGHT

U.S. TREASURY OBLIGATIONS

FAIL-SAFE RATING ON . . .

Safety: Treasury securities are absolutely the least risky that you can buy in the sense that principal and interest are backed by the full faith and credit of the U.S. government. In a pinch, the Federal Reserve System can create the money the Treasury would need to meet its obligations.

Income: Because the risk to principal and interest is nil, the rates paid on Treasury securities are not the highest available. The returns, for example, are less than on corporate obligations though the differences can be as small as a fraction of a percentage point.

Tax Status: Interest on Treasuries is subject to Federal income taxes, but is exempt from those of state and local governments.

Many people consider Treasury securities to be the ideal investment vehicle. Such issues satisfy their concern for safety of principal. And the returns that are received seem high — at the time of purchase, anyway. These investors don't always realize that inflation keeps eroding the true worth of their capital — often by as much as they earn in interest. In other words, they may not be making anything at all on their money; to the extent that they treat the interest as income and spend it, they are living off their savings.

As noted in the previous chapter, though, alert investors can minimize the impact of inflation by gearing their decisions to interest-rate swings — not infallibly, of course, but to an extent that can avoid being left at the starting gate when yields make a large or sustained move.

Not everyone buys Treasuries at the wrong time. There is still a substantial number of investors — individuals as well as professional — who find that such securities have a role to play. This is why the government can sell as much as $60 billion worth of Treasury issues a year to finance the debt generated by the large budget deficits. To the extent that the Reagan Administration can reduce spending, approach a balanced budget, and cut the inflation rate, interest rates will come down, too, and the recent record-high yields on Treasury securities will be a bonanza for investors who took them on; the returns would provide real, after-inflation yields that are extremely high by historical standards. So, if assured income is important to your well-being, there may still be a place for Treasuries in your investment scheme, providing that you time your purchases with care.

What kind of Treasuries to buy? To review the array for the record, the U.S. government issues a variety of securities, some sold for periods of only months or even days while others don't come due for decades. The maturities you choose should, of course, be related to your purpose at the time. Because the debt total is now in the trillion-dollar range, the Treasury is kept very busy, indeed, selling new issues to raise new money or refinancing — rolling over —

outstanding securities as they come due. Sometimes, the Treasury has to conduct sales of different obligations on three or even four days of a given week.

Let's take a closer look now at the kinds of issues the Treasury offers:

BILLS: These are short-term securities that come due in one year or less. They are sold in a minimum denomination of $10,000, and multiples of $5,000 beyond that. Every Monday, the Treasury auctions two sets of bills—one maturing in thirteen weeks, the other in twenty-six, for a weekly total that has climbed above $8 billion, most of which is to refinance bills coming due. Every four weeks, on a Thursday, it auctions bills due in fifty-two weeks. And at various times it sells cash-management bills which can run for a few days to as long as six months, depending on the particular need at the time. These bills are used to smooth out the irregular flow of revenue—with the Treasury borrowing when the tax take is especially light and paying off the bills when the inflow is heavy.

The auctions at which bills are sold are true auctions in every sense of the word. Banks, dealers, and investors literally bid for the amounts of these securities that they want. The Treasury then awards the bills, at first to those who bid the highest price—and the lowest interest cost—to the government; then it moves down the line, to those who bid successively lower prices, until the amount it wanted to sell has been reached. For individuals who don't feel qualified to figure a price for a numerical bid, there is still a way to participate in these actions. (See below on "How to Buy Treasury Securities.")

Treasury bills are an ideal short-term parking place for temporarily idle cash, money which is not yet ready for a permanent home. Corporations can keep tax payments and dividend distributions in bills, earning interest while waiting for the disbursement dates to arrive. As noted, investors who expect bond and note yields to go higher often prefer to "stay short" in bills or similar securities until the time comes to "lengthen out." They know that, should they want to get out or need the money before the bills mature, they can easily sell them at any time; the market for bills is huge and active. And, because bills have short maturities, the market risk of a big decline in price is relatively small. What's more, the return on bills can be high—even higher than on longer-term Treasuries at certain times.

To repeat a point made earlier, bills are sold on what's called a discount basis, and the discount rate is the one usually meant when talking about the bill rate. It reflects the fact that bills are sold by the Treasury at some amount below their face value; the investor gets the face amount when the bill comes due later, with the difference—the discount—being his interest. The discount rate is computed by dividing the *face amount* into the interest received and then converting it to an annual rate if the bill is of less than a year's maturity. Then there is one more step: Since banks historically computed interest on the basis of a convenient 360-day year, the discount rate also takes this into account. Thus, for a $10,000, 26-week bill auctioned for $9300 the discount rate would be 13.846%: $700 ÷ $10,000 = 7% × 360/182 days (to get the annual rate for the 26-week issue).

But the discount rate is not the true return on the investment. The true yield is something called the coupon equivalent yield. This is the interest actually received divided by the amount that is *actually invested* computed on a full-year basis. (For the same 26-week bill, it would be 15.095%: $700 ÷ $9300 × 365/182). The discount rate for Treasury bills should not be confused with the Federal Reserve's discount rate, which is a totally different animal.

NOTES: These are medium-term securities which mature in one to ten years. Those for less than three and a half years are sold in minimum amounts of $5,000; for all others, the minimum is $1,000. They pay interest semiannually. Some two-year notes are sold every month; a four- and a five-year issue is auctioned every quarter. In February, May, August, and November, the Treasury sells notes set to mature in three years or so, as well as seven-to-ten years in connection with quarterly financings to refund maturing issues and raise new cash.

Treasury notes usually appeal to investors who want fairly long-term securities, but are not ready to commit for twenty or thirty years. For example, insurance companies, which like to match maturities of securities with their needs to pay claims that their actuaries project will arise year by year, will invest in an array of notes maturing in successive years. Many individuals don't like to go beyond two or three years. Though they may recognize that they can always sell out in the market sooner, should they need the money, they don't like to face the bother or the market risks of having to accept a price less than they paid because of market-rate fluctuation.

You will generally get advance word of coming Treasury note auctions—and bond auctions, too—in many daily newspapers.

BONDS: These are securities which mature in more than ten years. Minimum denomination is $1,000. Maturities range as long as thirty years and in the future may go out as far as forty years. On many of the issues that don't fall due for many years, the Treasury reserves the right to call or redeem the bond on any interest payment date beginning five years before the final maturity date. Interest is paid semiannually. Bond sales are generally held around eight times a year, with twenty- and thirty-year maturities now the most commonly offered.

Bonds generally appeal to investors who

want to lock up what they consider to be attractive yields for as long as they can, to protect themselves against the necessity of reinvesting the principal from maturing issues at a time when rates could be low.

U.S. SAVINGS BONDS: Though most investors have all but forgotten that Savings Bonds exist, the Treasury still sells large amounts annually, mostly through its Payroll Savings Plan. It offers two types:

>   ***Series EE bonds*** (successors to the old E's) in denominations as little as $37.50 with a maturity value of $50. The interest earned is the difference between the issue price and the value of maturity nine years later. Buyers are free to cash them in at banks at any time after the first six months, though their rate of return increases the longer they hold. Individuals can buy up to $10,000 worth in any one year.

>   ***Series HH bonds***, which are sold at full face value for periods of ten years and come in registered form with checks mailed semi-annually. Minimum denomination is $500 with a maximum of $10,000 permitted each year.

Despite the authority to raise rates as much as 1% as often as twice a year, which was granted by Congress in 1980, the yields on Savings Bonds usually lag those available on savings certificates, money-market mutual-fund shares, and even the Treasury's own bills; shortly after the Treasury moved to implement its new authority, the gap was still as much as four percentage points.

Why do people continue to buy them? For one thing, that very low minimum on the EE's; what other investment requires so little? For another, savings bond interest is exempt from state and local income taxes; and Federal taxes can be deferred in the case of the EE's until they are redeemed, maybe after retirement, when the buyer's bracket is likely to be lower. Finally, automatic payroll deduction provides the only way that millions of Americans can make themselves save.

For others, though, especially those willing and able to take some time to examine attractive investment possibilities, EE and HH bonds make a nice birthday gift.

> Incidentally, Series E bonds that were issued before May 1941 no longer earn interest after May 1981. And those issued in successive years also cut off, year by year in May, after their fortieth year. So check the dates on your old bonds. If they are going to stop drawing interest, cash them in, if only to replace them with new ones.

How to buy Treasury Securities: Basically, there are two ways to purchase Treasury securities—directly from the Treasury at an auction, or in the open or so-called secondary market.

As mentioned earlier, the Treasury auctions bills every week. It announces the previous week precisely how much in bills it wishes to sell. Banks and bond dealers submit tenders, each offering to purchase a specified amount of bills at a specified price. As noted above, the Treasury awards bills to the highest bidders. Investors who don't feel comfortable deciding what to bid can submit noncompetitive tenders; they end up paying the average price of all the bids that the Treasury accepts from the big banks and dealers and professional investors.

You can get applications for the bill, note, and bond sales from:

> The Bureau of the Public Debt
> Securities Transactions Branch
> Room 2134 Main Treasury
> Washington, DC 20226

Or you can buy notes and bonds through your nearest Federal Reserve District Bank or branch. (A list appears at the end of this chapter.) Your bank can buy any of these

Treasuries for you, at a fee. Better not rely on the mails for receipt of the forms because the time between announcement and auction can be too short.

> To purchase a security, your tender must be received by 1:30 P.M. Eastern Time on the day of the sale. Note and bond sales dates vary. To find out if bonds or notes are currently being offered, you can telephone the Treasury in Washington at (202) 287-4100

If you are submitting a tender for a bill, you must enclose a certified or cashier's check for the full face amount, $10,000 or more. The Treasury will rebate the discount to you—that is, your interest—by check through the mail after the rate has been determined. Checks should be made out to the Bureau of the Public Debt or to your Federal Reserve Bank, whichever you use. You will not receive your Treasury bill in the mail—merely a notice that an account has been opened in your name on the government's books. When the bill matures, you will automatically get a check for its full face amount.

Tenders for notes and bonds must also be paid for in full at the time that individuals subscribe (Banks and other financial institutions are still allowed to make only 5% deposits.) Again, make checks payable to the Bureau of the Public Debt. They need not be certified or cashier's checks.

> With notes and bonds, you have the option of getting your security in *registered* or *bearer* form. If it is registered, the Treasury will automatically send you your semiannual interest payments. If it is in bearer form, the security will come with coupons attached. Twice a year, on the specified payment date, you clip a coupon and deposit it like a check.

When you buy an outstanding bond or note in the open market, you must pay not only the market price and the commission to a bank or broker but also any accrued interest that the previous holder may have earned but not yet collected. For example, if in April you purchase a security on which a semiannual interest payment is scheduled to be made in May, you must compensate the holder in cash for the five months of interest he is giving up to you. Of course, you get this back when you get your interest payment—for the full six months, not just the briefer period for which you owned the security.

Though Treasury securities are considered conservative investments in themselves, they do offer opportunities for active speculation. Banks and brokers will sometimes lend as much as 90% of, say, a bond or note's value, holding on to the securities as collateral. If the issue's price rises significantly in a fairly short period, the gain can be a substantial percentage of the original investment.

> **For example:** Suppose you bought $100,000 of ten-year notes at par. You put up $10,000 and borrow the rest. If the price jumps three points in a month, you have a gross profit of $3,000. To be sure, you have some costs that must be offset against this. There are the brokerage commissions and your cost in interest on that $90,000 loan; it would be the difference between the, say, 15% you would have to pay the bank and the 10% you would be earning on the notes—or 5%. (Apply the 5% to the $90,000, then divide by 12 to get the cost for a single month: $4,500 ÷ 12 = $375.) Add in commissions of about $75 and you come up with total expenses of $450, leaving a net profit of $2,550 on your $10,000 investment—or 25½%. Annualize that by multiplying by 12 and you could claim a rate of return of better than 300% a year.

But note that the deal can cut both ways. Suppose the market *dropped* three points; you would suffer a *loss* of $3,000 plus the interest costs and the brokerage commissions. In other words, it's a very risky business. You have to be right in your projections—and not just over a year or more, as in the case of someone who buys a note outright and can afford to sit through the ups and downs of a rapidly fluctuating market. To come out ahead in this sort of speculation, you have to pinpoint your timing—and, as noted in the previous chapter—that is far from easy to do.

Speculating in Treasury bill futures is another rapidly growing area that will be discussed in Chapter Eighteen— on Commodities.

FEDERAL RESERVE OFFICES

ATLANTA
404-586-8500; 104 Marietta Street, N.W., Atlanta, Georgia 30303
Birmingham Branch
205-252-3141; 1801 Fifth Avenue, North (P.O. Box 10447) Birmingham, Alabama 35202
Jacksonville Branch
904-632-4400; 515 Julia Street, Jacksonville, Florida 33231
Miami Branch
305-445-6281; 3770 S.W. 8th Street, Coral Gables, Florida 33134 (P.O. Box 520847, Miami, Florida 33152)
Nashville Branch
615-259-4006; 301 Eighth Avenue, North, Nashville, Tennessee 37203
New Orleans Branch
504-586-1505; 525 St. Charles Avenue (P.O. Box 61630) New Orleans, Louisiana 70161

BOSTON
617-973-3000; 600 Atlantic Avenue, Boston, Massachusetts 02106
Lewiston Office
207-784-2381; 1775 Lisbon Road, Lewiston, Maine 04240
Windsor Locks Office
203-623-2561; Windsor Locks, Connecticut 06096

CHICAGO
312-322-5322; 230 South La Salle Street (P.O. Box 834) Chicago, Illinois 60690
Des Moines Office
515-284-8800; 616 Tenth Street, Des Moines, Iowa 50309 (P.O. Box 1903, Des Moines, Iowa 50306)

Detroit Branch
313-961-6880; 160 Fort Street, West (P.O. Box 1059) Detroit, Michigan
48231
Indianapolis Branch
317-635-4766; 41 E. Washington Street, Indianapolis, Indiana 46204 (P.O.
Box 20208, Indianapolis, Indiana 46206)
Milwaukee Office
414-276-2323; 304 East State Street, Milwaukee, Wisconsin 53202 (P.O.
Box 361, Milwaukee, Wisconsin 53201)

CLEVELAND
216-241-2800; 1455 East Sixth Street (P.O. Box 6387) Cleveland, Ohio
44101
Cincinnati Branch
513-721-4787; 150 East Fourth Street (P.O. Box 999) Cincinnati, Ohio
45201
Columbus Office
614-846-7050; 965 Kingsmill Parkway, Columbus, Ohio 43229 (P.O. Box
189, Columbus, Ohio 43216)
Pittsburgh Office
412-261-7800; 717 Grant Street (P.O. Box 867) Pittsburgh, Pennsylvania
15230

DALLAS
214-651-6111; 400 South Akard Street (Station K) Dallas, Texas 75222
El Paso Branch
915-544-4730; 301 East Main Street (P.O. Box 100) El Paso, Texas
79999
Houston Branch
713-659-4433; 1701 San Jacinto Street (P.O. Box 2578) Houston, Texas
77001
San Antonio Branch
512-224-2141; 126 East Nueva Street (P.O. Box 1471) San Antonio, Texas
78295

KANSAS CITY
816-881-2000; 925 Grand Avenue (Federal Reserve Station) Kansas City,
Missouri 64198
Denver Branch
303-293-4020; 1020 16th Street (Terminal Annex, P.O. Box 5228) Denver, Colorado 80217
Oklahoma City Branch
405-235-1721; 226 Northwest Third Street (P.O. Box 25129) Oklahoma
City, Oklahoma 73125
Omaha Branch
402-341-3610; 1702 Dodge Street, Omaha, Nebraska 68102

MINNEAPOLIS
612-340-2345; 250 Marquette Avenue, Minneapolis, Minnesota 55480
Helena Branch
406-442-3860; 400 North Park Avenue, Helena, Montana 59601

NEW YORK
212-79\-5000; 33 Liberty Street (Federal Reserve P.O. Station) New York,
New York 10045
Buffalo Branch
716-849-5000; 160 Delaware Avenue (P.O. Box 961) Buffalo, New York
14240

PHILADELPHIA
215-574-6000; 100 North 6th Street, Philadelphia, Pennsylvania 19106
(P.O. Box 66, Philadelphia, Pennsylvania 19105)

RICHMOND
804-643-1250; 100 North Ninth Street (P.O. Box 27622) Richmond, Virginia 23219
Baltimore Branch
301-539-6552; 114-120 East Lexington Street (P.O. Box 1378) Baltimore,
Maryland 21203
Charlotte Branch
704-373-0220; 401 South Tryon Street (P.O. Box 300) Charlotte, North
Carolina 28230
Charleston Office
304-345-8020; 1200 Airport Road (P.O. Box 2309) Charleston, West Virginia 25311
Columbia Office
803-772-1940; 1624 Browning Road (P.O. Box 132) Columbia, South Carolina 29202

ST. LOUIS
314-444-8444; 411 Locust Street (P.O. Box 442) St.Louis, Missouri
63166
Little Rock Branch
501-372-5451; 325 West Capitol Avenue (P.O. Box 1261) Little Rock,
Arkansas 72203
Louisville Branch
502-587-7351; 410 South Fifth Street (P.O. Box 32710) Louisville, Ken-
tucky 40232
Memphis Branch
901-523-7171; 200 N. Main Street (P.O. Box 407) Memphis, Tennessee
38101

SAN FRANCISCO
415-544-2000; 400 Sansome Street (P.O. 7702) San Francisco, California 94120

Los Angeles Branch
213-683-8323; 409 West Olympic Boulevard (P.O. Box 2077) Los Angeles, California 90051

Portland Branch
503-221-5900; 915 S.W. Stark Street (P.O. Box 3436) Portland, Oregon 97208

Salt Lake City Branch
801-355-3131; 120 South Street (P.O. Box 780) Salt Lake City, Utah 84110

Seattle Branch
206-442-1376; 1015 Second Avenue (P.O. Box 3567, Terminal Annex) Seattle, Washington 98124

CHAPTER NINE

FEDERAL-AGENCY ISSUES

FAIL-SAFE RATING ON . . .

Safety: They are virtually on a par with securities of the U.S. Treasury itself.

Income: Yields are usually a fraction of a percentage point higher than those on Treasury securities.

Tax Status: All are subject to Federal income taxes, but some are exempt from those at the state and local levels.

For conservative people who like the safety of Treasury securities but prefer to avoid the greater risks that go with the higher yields on other investments, there is a very comfortable compromise — Federal-agency issues.

Over the decades, the Federal government has created or sponsored dozens of agencies to carry out a variety of programs or to further a national priority, often in agriculture or housing. In recent years, many of these have acquired independent or quasi-independent corporate status.

But, whether independent or still a part of the Federal establishment, these agencies rely on the public markets rather than tax dollars for their funds. Just like commercial enterprises, they sell bonds, debentures, and notes — and sometimes stock — in a range of denominations and maturities. Some require such large minimum investments that they are largely purchased by institutions. But others are well within the reach of the average investor. And, in increasing numbers, smaller investors and savers are finding these securities very attractive because they do combine some of the best safety and tax features of direct Treasury obligations with somewhat higher yields that are closer to those of the best corporate securities.

Let's first take a look at what makes Federal-agency securities attractive in general. Later, we will examine some of the more popular of these issues to give you a good sampling of what is available. *Much of their appeal lies in the fact that most are every bit as safe as Treasuries* for the very simple reason that they carry an implicit or explicit government guarantee. Even those which carry no explicit guarantee (and most of them don't) are usually regarded as being virtually default-proof. These agencies are so closely associated with the government and its programs that they can be considered part of the U.S. government. Congress would never allow them to default on their obligations.

Indeed, none ever has, and it is highly doubtful that any — even those which are officially "private" enterprises—will ever come close. For one thing, these independent agencies usually have the right to borrow directly from the U.S. Treasury, if necessary, to pay off the interest and principal of their obligations. So, the worst that could ever happen is that interest payments could be delayed. But even that isn't likely, even under the worst of economic conditions. In effect, then, these are perfect substitutes for Treasury issues.

As a general rule, agencies will yield anywhere from a few hundredths of one percentage point to a full point more than Treasuries, depending on the maturity of the issue and the amount of money the agencies need to borrow. (And they can be that much below high-quality corporate securities.) In times of sharply rising or falling interest rates, spreads can widen or narrow.

Why any difference at all in yield? For all their being as good as Treasuries, they aren't the same, and some big institutional investors that go by the book don't formally recognize them as quite the same. Then, too, the agency markets aren't as big as the Treasury's, so that particular issues aren't as "tradable"—that is, don't have as many other investors waiting to buy and sell. And that means a shading of prices, either way, which in turn affects yields and yield spreads.

You may find that at times you can get no higher yield on an agency security than on some Treasury issues. In such admittedly rare cases, you can have the slightly extra advantage of a Treasury without any need to accept a lower yield.

The partial tax exemption that some agency issues enjoy varies from state to state. If you live in a state with no income tax, it is worth nothing to you. But if you live in one with a high income-tax rate—such as New York—the exemption can make the after-tax yield on an agency issue about equal to that on a high-grade corporate bond.

For example: Assume that you live in a state where the income-tax rate is 10% for someone in your bracket. You would do as well as with an agency security which pays 9% interest as you would with a corporate bond paying 10%.

Now let's take a look at some of the agencies we've been talking about and the kind of securities they offer. First, some government-sponsored agencies:

The Federal National Mortgage Association (Fannie Mae) is a private corporation, though it began life under the auspices of the Federal government, which still has a say in who runs it and how it operates. Fannie Mae raises money in the bond and money markets, selling its securities to banks, insurance companies, and others. It uses the money to buy existing Federal Housing Administration-guaranteed and Veterans Administration-insured, as well, on conventional mortgages from lenders. The idea is to keep pumping money back into these institutuions so they can make new mortgage commitments. In effect, the Association is a conduit for channeling funds from the bond and money markets into housing. Fannie Mae sells debentures regularly — at least once every three months and occasionally more often. They are sold in minimum denominations of $10,000, with increments of $5,000 thereafter. Interest is taxable by states.

The Federal Home Loan Mortgage Corporation (Freddie Mac) buys conventional mortgages — rather than the FHA-VA–insured type — from banks, savings and loan associations, and mortgage-bankers, to keep loan money flowing into the home-building market. It gets the funds to do so by selling to investors Participation Certificates in pools of mortgages that the Corporation assembles from its purchased holdings; the Certificates are guaranteed as to principal and interest by Freddie Mac itself, rather than the Federal government, so income is taxable at all levels — by Federal, state, and local governments. Minimum denominations are $100,000. The mortgages in the pools — and therefore the Certificates—have an average remaining life of six to eight years.

The Federal Home Loan Banks sell notes and bonds to raise money to lend to savings banks and savings and loan associations. The securities are not directly guaranteed by the U.S. government but are backed by the twelve Federal Home Loan Banks, which can borrow from the U.S. Treasury. Interest payments on the securities are exempt from state and local taxes. The securities are sold in minimum denominations of $10,000 with increments of $5,000. The banks normally issue new bonds every three months.

The Federal Farm Credit Banks are three separate agencies that function in tandem—the Banks for Cooperatives, the Federal Intermediate Credit Banks, and the Federal Land Banks, together comprising the Farm Credit System. They all raise funds to reloan to the farm sector or for various purposes—to farmers, cooperatives, and commercial banks in farm areas. The three agencies issue their securities jointly. Each month, the System sells notes which mature in six or nine months in minimum denominations of $5,000, half the minimum of a Treasury bill. Farm Credit also issues bonds in denominations as low as $1,000, usually quarterly. Interest payments are exempt from state and local taxes. The securities are not directly guaranteed by the government but usually are backed by collateral of some kind, often mortgages on farm property.

> The government-sponsored agencies listed above provide the bulk of the securities bought and sold in the agency market. But government agencies themselves also guarantee privately issued securities which may be attractive to individual investors.

The Government National Mortgage Association (Ginnie Mae) is the best-known guarantor. It is an arm of the Department of Housing and Urban Development. Its function is to generate funds for new mortgages by guaranteeing so-called pass-through securities. These represent shares in pools of FHA-VA mortgages assembled by private lenders such as banks, savings banks, savings and loan associations, or mortgage bankers. The interest and repayments of principal are "passed through" to investors; in other words, the investor gets the same sort of amortization as any mortgage-holder would. Because some of the mortgages in the pool began paying off a while ago—and because others will be paid off before their span has run—the maturity of the pass-through certificates can be as short as six or eight years; effectively, then, they are like six- or eight-year bonds or notes. The minimum denomination for a pass-through security is $25,000.

> Ginnie Mae-guaranteed pass-through securities are backed by the full faith and credit of the U.S. government, because the Association is regarded as a unit of the government. They are treated like Treasury securities for tax purposes and so are not subject to state and local taxes. These days, brokerage firms are selling shares in unit investment trusts which invest in these securities in much the same way that a mutual fund will invest your money in common stocks. (See Chapter Thirteen.) Such shares come in minimum denominations of as little as $1,000 each. There is also a sales commission of perhaps 3%, plus a small administrative fee.

The Federal Small Business Administration guarantees loans made by banks to small companies for up to 90% of the face amount. When the banks have to raise cash, they may sell the insured portions of such loans to brokers, who resell them to investors. Yields are about as high as those available on good-quality corporate issues and the maturities average about 7½ years. But the guarantee feature makes such investments virtually risk-free—on a par with insured savings certificates.

There are some aspects of these loans that some investors might consider drawbacks. For one thing, the market for them is small, so it isn't always easy to buy or sell. For another, the minimum amounts required to invest are usually $20,000 or more, though loans of $10,000—even $5,000—are sometimes available.

The Federal Maritime Administration guarantees ship mortgages in much the same way. Minimum denominations for such securities is $250,000.

How to Buy: As a rule it is easy to purchase any agency security through a securities broker. If he is a member of the underwriting group that is selling a new issue for the agency, you pay no commission. Many banks will also make such purchases for you, for a fee. Major newspapers often carry announcements of coming offerings, though at times very little notice is given by the issuing agency. Usually, it is best to let your bank or broker know you are interested in purchasing a new issue when it is offered so that he can call you when an offering is first announced.

If you buy in the secondary market—that is, issues that came out previously and are already outstanding—you normally pay a commission or fee just as with any other purchase of securities through a bank or broker.

Some sixty brokerage houses, including almost all of the majors, deal in SBA loans generated by the 700 banks active in this market. SBA has a list of these firms. Write to the Director of Secondary Markets, SBA, 26 Federal Plaza, New York, NY 10028. Ask your bank if it is one of those making and selling SBA loans; dealing direct could save on the commission.

CHAPTER TEN

TAX-EXEMPT STATE AND LOCAL GOVERNMENT SECURITIES

FAIL-SAFE RATING ON . . .

Safety: So-called municipal notes and bonds range in quality from the very highest—almost comparable to Treasuries—to some that you might not be comfortable owning, though defaults by state and local government units are rare.

Income: In absolute levels, the rates of return paid are lower than no-risk Treasuries yield. But . . .

Tax Status: The exemption from Federal income taxes—and often from state levies, as well—can yield higher-bracket taxpayers some of the highest after-tax returns available anywhere.

Investing in tax-exempt securities—those issued by state and local governments and their agencies—was once reserved for only the very wealthy. They were the only ones on whom the tax bite was high enough to warrant the purchase of these relatively low-yielding debt obligations. But, as inflation pushed an ever-larger portion of the population into ever-higher tax brackets, tax-exempt state and local government issues, or municipal securities as they are very commonly called, have become a staple investment for many in the middle and upper-middle income groups— people who have had to pay combined state and Federal taxes at rates of 30% or more. And now, as we'll see below, there are even ways to eliminate a major drawback to such issues: the danger of being locked into fixed-rate issues as inflation drives interest rates higher.

Still, the world of municipal finance is mysterious and in some ways baffling for many investors. They find themselves faced with a bewildering array of securities issued by literally thousands of states, cities, counties, school districts, bridge or airport authorities, and other bodies. Some are backed by the full faith and credit—and the taxing power— of the issuing unit; supposedly, they can always raise taxes to get the money to make the payments of interest and principal. But others rely only on the revenues generated by specific projects or services to meet the payments.

Though as a rule municipal securities rank behind only Treasury and Federal-agency debt in safety, they are unlike these obligations in that the quality is not uniform; there is a fairly wide degree of variance in the standing of municipal securities—so much so, in fact, that municipal obligations are quality rated. (See below for a description of the rating system.) Nevertheless, as a group, municipals have an enviable safety record, despite the much-publicized troubles in New York City and Cleveland. Note that, even in the Great Depression, some 98% of all municipal securities continued making interest payments. And most of those which did default eventually satisfied their obligations.

The combination of safety and tax advan-

tages municipals offer goes far to explain why they play such a large role in the holdings of so many investors. Their charms are enhanced by the fact that municipal securities' interest payments are not only exempt from Federal taxes, but may be exempt from state and local income taxes, as well, usually only if the buyer is a resident of the state or political subdivision which issued the securities. Depending on your tax bracket, you could readily get as much or more in after-tax income from a municipal bond as you would from a corporate bond carrying a yield several percentage points higher.

Under any given set of tax laws, tax experts can prepare a table that shows just what someone in your tax bracket would have to earn on a fully taxable investment to equal a range of tax-exempt yields. With the tax laws scheduled to undergo successive changes over the next several years, in ways that are not yet clear or certain, no one table will be applicable for very long during this transition period. So the table that follows — that in effect at the start of 1981 — would give only a rough indication of the kind of tax savings (or after-tax yields) that tax-exempt securities can provide. Should you want a precise calculation at any particular time, ask your broker for a table based on the law in effect at the time; chances are he'll have some around — or will be able to get one for you quickly.

Under the table being used herewith for illustration, if you are in the 49% tax bracket, for example, a municipal bond yielding 8% gives almost as much after-tax income as a 16% yield from a taxable source — even more when state or local tax savings are considered. In the 70% tax bracket — and brackets go that high on investment income — you'd have to earn nearly 27% from a taxable source to equal the after-tax yield of an 8% municipal. The table that follows shows what taxpayers in various brackets would have to earn on a taxable security to equal various tax-exempt yields.

USING THE TAX TABLE

The tax rate you use to figure the taxable-equivalent yield is your marginal tax rate—that is, your highest bracket-rate. It is not the percentage of your income you paid in taxes, but the percentage of the last dollar of investment income you earn that you will have to pay. A married couple with a taxable income of $48,000 normally paid $13,798 or about 28% of their income in Federal taxes under the schedule in effect in 1980. They pay 14% on the first $4,000, 16% on the next $2,000 and so on. On everything above $45,800 they are paying 49% on the dollar—and would on any more up to $60,000. So 49% is their marginal tax rate and the rate they use in this calculation.

But if that same couple had a taxable income of more than $60,000, they would have two marginal tax rates—50% on all wage and salary income and anywhere from 50% to 70% on so-called unearned income such as investment income.

How much is a municipal bond's tax exemption worth to you? Find your income tax bracket on the chart on Page 101 and read across.

Municipal securities come in a range of maturities, much like Treasuries. Some are issued for very short periods; tax-anticipation notes of two or three months or so are often sold to tide a government unit over until the tax deadline brings revenues flooding in, at which time the notes are redeemed. Other notes can be written to come due in a year or so. Many banks, corporations, and other investors who need temporary parking places for idle cash, find such short-term issues attractive. The interest rates they offer may be relatively modest—though still worthwhile after taxes.

Tax-exempts that are designated to finance long-term

taxable income joint return in thousands of dollars	% tax bracket	4.00%	4.50%	5.00%	5.50%	6.00%	6.50%	7.00%	7.50%	8.00%	8.50%	9.00%
20- 24	28%	5.56%	6.25%	6.94%	7.64%	8.33%	9.03%	9.72%	10.42%	11.11%	11.81%	12.50%
24- 29	32	5.88	6.62	7.35	8.09	8.82	9.56	10.29	11.03	11.76	12.50	13.24
29- 35	37	6.35	7.14	7.94	8.73	9.52	10.32	11.11	11.90	12.70	13.49	14.29
35- 45	43	7.02	7.89	8.77	9.65	10.53	11.40	12.28	13.16	14.04	14.91	15.79
45- 60	49	7.84	8.82	9.80	10.78	11.76	12.75	13.73	14.71	15.68	16.67	17.65
60- 85	54	8.70	9.78	10.87	11.96	13.04	14.13	15.22	16.30	17.39	18.48	19.57
85-109	59	9.76	10.98	12.20	13.41	14.63	15.85	17.07	18.29	19.51	20.73	21.95
109-162	64	11.11	12.50	13.89	15.28	16.67	18.06	19.44	20.83	22.22	23.61	25.00
162-215	68	12.50	14.06	15.63	17.19	18.75	20.31	21.88	23.44	25.00	26.56	28.12
Over 215	70	13.33	15.00	16.67	18.33	20.00	21.67	23.33	25.00	26.67	28.33	30.00

Computed from Tax Tables Effective January 1, 1979, which would no longer be applicable if tax cuts are voted in 1981.

projects—sewers, waterworks, bridges, or schools—
generally run from five to twenty years or so.

These days, less than half of municipal securities are so-
called general obligation bonds or notes—those that are
backed by the full faith and credit of the issuing entity. The
so-called revenue bonds, backed by receipts from a specific
tax or toll, are now being issued in increasing volume.

Hospitals are included among those offering tax-
exempt bonds with attractive yields. In effect, they enjoy a
Federal subsidy that helps keep down the cost of care to
Medicare and Medicaid patients. But investing in their securities demands careful consideration of the institution's
financial health, which in turn depends on its ability to
charge enough to enough patients to meet its expenses and
its interest charges.

Local public housing authorities issue securities that are a kind of hybrid. They are sold to finance low-
rent public housing projects and are backed by the full faith
and credit of the U.S. government. This backing enables the
issuer to sell its securities at a lower rate—and that is a sort
of Federal subsidy to the local authorities.

**All other things equal, general obligations
yield a little less than revenue bonds.** But,
though a revenue bond by definition does not have the
same full backing as a general-obligation issue, it may still
be as good or even a better investment. It all depends on the
underlying quality. Bonds of the highly successful New Jer-
sey Turnpike Authority are a better risk than those of some
financially shaky cities. Because of this, the Turnpikes may
actually yield less.

In recent years, the danger of being caught with what
could turn out to be relatively low yields as interest rates
keep rising has made many investors hesitate to take advantage of the tax-exemption feature. But some borrowers are
now offering innovative features that work to nullify this
drawback—variable-rate tax-exempt issues (and corporate
and real-estate securities as well). Local governments began
the trend with the bond issues they sponsor that allow pri-

vate corporations to raise money at the favorable tax-exempt rates for industrial development or pollution control. The principle, though, can be applied to tax-exempt issues generally.

> Initially, such bonds—sold on behalf of companies like U.S. Steel or the Cleveland Electric Illuminating—offered yields that are established percentages of those available on Treasury securities; the ratios are based on past relationships among the yields on particular companies' bonds, Treasuries, and tax-exempts. Then, the yields are adjusted regularly, as those on Treasuries move up or down. As a result, the bonds always tend to trade around par. So the buyer's initial investment is intact, while he always enjoys current rates of return.

As noted, this sort of bond is relatively new. But it seems bound to catch on if interest-rate fluctuations continue to be so broad—as is expected. Investors will want to give such issues serious consideration—as ways to enjoy the benefits of tax exemption and preserve their capital, too. Ask your broker to alert you to such issues—especially some in your state.

Most tax-exempt bonds are issued in serial form—that is, the bonds come due at annual intervals. For example, a state might issue $100 million in revenue bonds and arrange the offering so that some of the bonds mature in 1981, some in 1982 and so on until the entire issue is retired in, say, 2004; each of the maturities would carry successively higher yields. Some tax-exempts, though, are "term" bonds—issued for a uniform period of, say, twenty years. Fairly often, a state or local government will sell a combination of some term and some serial bonds.

HOW TO JUDGE QUALITY: Several private companies evaluate—or "rate"—tax-exempt securities (and corporates, too) for their ability to meet obligations. They analyze quality—essentially, the ability to make the interest payments and redeem the principal—from the point of view of taxable property base, already outstanding debt, outlook for the community or project, etc. Here is a brief rundown of what municipal-bond ratings mean, using the Standard & Poor's rating system.

First, though, one important point to bear in mind: These safety ratings should be used primarily as guidelines. They can make it easier for you to select an acceptable investment by allowing you to eliminate everything below a certain rating level—say AA. But you should still exercise care and discretion in selecting bonds within the AA and AAA classifications.

- *AAA—These are prime municipals.* The rating agency is saying that, in its professional judgment, the issuers of these bonds have the strongest capacity for meeting interest and principal payments. When applied to general-obligation bonds, the rating means the issuers are less vulnerable to dips in over-all economic activity than others; they have relatively small debt burdens and are generally well managed. When applied to revenue bonds it means that receipts are strong and stable and more than sufficient to meet obligations to bondholders. Management is also thought to be strong.

- *AA—These are very high-grade municipals.* The rating agency regards them as safe investments because the issuer has the ability to meet debt-service payments in a timely fashion even under adverse economic conditions. They are very close to AAA bonds in safety and stability, and often the dividing line between the two categories is so fuzzy that one rating agency will rate a bond AAA while another rates it AA.

- *A—These are still investment-grade bonds* and are still regarded as safe investments. Principal and interest payments are considered secure. However, there are some reasons to be a little cautious. Perhaps the debt burden is somewhat higher than it should be or the municipality's economic base may not be quite as strong. Or the area or facility may be more vulnerable to swings in overall economic activity than those of higher-rater issuers. As a rule, this is the lowest-grade bond we would recommend for investors for whom stability and certainty of income are primary goals.

• ***BBB—These are a clear cut below the others.*** They usually show more than one of the weaknesses referred to in the discussion of A-rated issues above. Although these are still regarded as investment-grade issues, in the sense that they are legal investments for trusts and financial institutions, they are not generally recommended except to those willing to accept a somewhat higher degree of risk to get a higher return.

• ***BB and below—These issues are quite speculative.*** The farther down you go in the ratings, the more speculative the issues become. Not only are the yields of the securities affected by interest-rate levels and rate movements generally, but they are also heavily influenced by overall economic activity, to say nothing of the immediate fortunes of the issuer. As a practical matter, there is a limit to the degree to which a government entity can raise taxes to meet obligations. Though few BB or lower bonds go into default, the risk is there. So these issues do not meet the criteria for Fail-Safe Investing.

> Some tax-exempt bond issuers carry private insurance that guarantees the payment of principal and interest if the issuer can't. Or the investor can buy such protection himself, often if the minimun amount of bonds is $50,000. Either way, the extra protection could permit the purchase of a somewhat lower-quality bond without significant sacrifice of safety, overall.

HOW TO BUY: Any stockbroker can buy tax-exempt notes and bonds for you on commission. Blocks of $25,000 worth or more are usually easier to sell; for amounts less than that, there may have to be a price concession of a fraction of a point or more. But, generally, these securities are available in minimum units of $1,000.

There is a very convenient way to buy tax-exempt issues that has proven highly popular in recent years—through mutual funds or so-called unit investment trusts. These are established by large brokerage houses and investment institutions that sell shares, usually in $1,000 units, and invest the proceeds in municipal bonds. The unit trusts retain the bonds as a single unchanged package until they come due, while mutual funds buy and sell issues from time to time, trying to adapt to changes in market conditions. Either way, the investor gets the benefit of tax exemption and the risk is minimized because it is spread among, say, a score of issues. Among the mutual funds, the no-loads—those charging no sales commission—deserve special consideration. Some tax-exempt mutual funds and unit trusts take out bond insurance to cover their holdings.

CHAPTER ELEVEN

CORPORATE BONDS AND NOTES

FAIL-SAFE RATING ON . . .

Safety: Corporate debt securities are ranked in safety after those of the Federal, state, and local governments. But that doesn't mean they are risky in an absolute sense — though some corporate issues may be more so than others and the differences can be critically important.

Income: Because of the moderately greater risk to principal and interest, as compared with government and agency securities, corporate issues pay moderately higher interest rates.

Tax status: Interest on corporates is fully taxable at the Federal and state-local levels.

Inflation is exerting such constant pressure to obtain higher yields on one's assets that investors — especially those needing assured income — can't ignore corporate bonds and notes. The returns can be very rewarding, if these securities can be acquired when rates seem to be near a peak. Returns above 13% have not been uncommon recently, even with risks kept low.

As most investors know, there are basically two ways a corporation in the United States can raise money from external sources — by selling its stock or by borrowing. For most serious investors, both avenues are important but, in this chapter, the emphasis will be on corporate debt securities. (See Chapter Thirteen for a discussion of stocks.)

Here are the basic kinds of debt issues that corporations offer:

BONDS: These are debt securities usually issued to finance long-range, expensive projects such as new factories, office buildings, and equipment. There are really two types: mortgage bonds and debentures. A mortgage bond, as the name implies, is backed by a specific asset or group of assets such as the building or the equipment the money is being used to finance. A debenture, on the other hand, is more like an unsecured loan. It is backed by the good name and general creditworthiness of the borrowing corporation. Both are long-term instruments, usually maturing in twenty to thirty years. They normally pay interest semiannually.

They are usually "callable." In other words, the issuing company has the right to redeem the bonds after a certain period of years, but prior to their stated maturity, by paying the holders a premium price. Companies do this so they can borrow during periods of high interest rates, while in effect reserving the option to redeem and reissue securities later on when rates are lower. Even if it has to pay a premium to redeem or call in its bonds early, the issuing company can often save substantial amounts of money later by refinancing.

For example, XYZ Corp. issues $100 million in bonds today at 10% interest. Its annual interest payments to bondholders amount to $10 million. Let's suppose that, a few years later, the prevailing level of interest rates for companies like XYZ Corp. has declined to 8% and, under the terms of its offering XYZ has the right to call the bond at a price of 110% (par plus one year's interest). But even if it has to borrow $110 million to retire the issue, it will only have to pay $8.8 million in annual interest, a savings of $1.2 million every year.

So investors who purchase long-term corporate bonds in high-interest-rate periods are vulnerable to having their securities called for redemption. To help make their bonds more attractive, corporations usually have to include a call-protection feature in their bonds. This just means that the company guarantees not to exercise its option to call the bonds for a stated number of years—that is, before the investor can get some benefit.

In the case of **public utilities**, call protection is usually only five years.

Industrial corporations usually grant ten-year call protection. That, by the way, is one reason industrial bonds frequently carry a lower yield than similarly rated utility issues. But they are also scarcer and not subject to regulatory control by rate-making bodies.

Some industrial companies also have sinking-fund provisions. The corporation, through a trustee, gradually redeems all or part of the outstanding issue prior to maturity, paying for the bonds out of the sinking fund it establishes at the time the bonds are issued and into which it makes regular payments. The trustee may simply purchase the bonds in the open market. But sometimes the specific bonds called in are determined by lot; yours could be among them. You can always use the money you receive from the redemption to reinvest in similar bonds—even bonds of the same issue that haven't yet been called.

Corporate bonds generally appeal to the same long-term investors who buy Treasury bonds. Insurance companies and pension funds may choose corporates because they get a better yield with a risk that is slightly — but acceptably — higher.

Yankee bonds—securities issued in the United States by foreign governments or government-sponsored enterprises — trade much like corporate bonds; normally, if the country is a major industrial nation, they carry a very high rating — AAA or AA. In general, they are thought to be very safe long-term investments. But, because the issuers are not as easy to keep track of, the bonds often carry a slightly higher yield than comparably rated domestic corporate issues. Interest payments are fully taxable.

Investors can also buy shares in bond funds, usually packaged by brokerage houses and available in units of as little as $1,000. The underwriters can offer high yields — higher than corporate bonds you would buy directly — because they mingle some lower-rated bonds in the fund portfolio. This gives a higher average yield, but the fact that there are also other, higher-rated issues behind your money spreads — and minimizes — the risk somewhat.

NOTES: The major difference between bonds and notes issued by a corporation is the maturity — the length of time for which they are sold. Notes generally are issued for ten years or less. They are a favored method of raising money for banks and finance companies and are also used by non-financial corporations, especially when interest rates are high; notes usually carry a somewhat lower rate of interest and don't lock the borrower into paying high rates for so long. A few have sinking-fund provisions. Call-protection varies with the period for which the note is issued.

Corporate notes appeal to the same kinds of investors who might buy Treasuries of similar maturities, but who give more weight to the greater yield than to the slightly greater risk.

As is the case with municipal securities, not every corporate issue carries the same degree of risk. Indeed, many investors would feel more comfortable holding certain high-grade corporate securities than many municipal bonds. As with municipals, the difference in yield between one corporate bond and another may reflect scarcity and the market's assessment of the relative degree of safety of the two securities. Call-protection is also a factor.

Also, like municipals, almost every new bond that comes to market carries a rating from one or both of the major bond-rating agencies, Standard & Poor's or Moody's. Their technicians weigh a corporation's inherent soundness in terms of its economic power, already outstanding debt, net worth, income stream, and other factors. The ratings work the same as for tax-exempts; in general, the higher the rating, the safer the bond is thought to be. An issue that carries a Triple-A rating from one of these rating agencies is likely to pay a lower yield than one that carries a Double-A rating, everything else being equal.

Here in a nutshell is what the ratings mean (using Standard & Poor's designations).

• *AAA—This is the highest rating that can be given.* It designates a top-quality issue, a blue chip, which offers the investor the highest degree of safety. The rating agency is saying it believes that the company has the financial strength to continue paying interest on its obligations through even the toughest economic conditions. But, of course, the prices of these securities still move in response to general market interest-rate changes.

• *AA—These are next in line in safety.* They are very high grade and differ only slightly from AAA issues in safety. Indeed, different analysts might disagree on whether certain borderline cases should be in one classification or the other. Their prices, too, move primarily with interest rates generally.

• *A—These are still conservative,* investment-grade obligations though clearly not in the same class with the two top grades. Their interest and principal payments are regarded as safe. Again, price changes reflect mostly changes in the level of interest rates.

• *BBB—These are medium-grade issues.* At

this point, economic and business conditions become important determinants in the outlook for the company—and the bond. Some people regard these obligations as essentially safe; but many others prefer to look elsewhere.

Anything below a BBB rating should be considered speculative. The degree of speculative risk is all that is in question. A prolonged period of economic hardship would leave in doubt the ability of the issuers to meet interest and principal payments.

In general, the ratings are the best guide the average investor has to the relative degree of safety of corporate-debt securities. But you shouldn't rely on them absolutely. A company could still run into sudden trouble that even the raters can't foresee.

Some sophisticated investors prefer to buy lower-rated corporate issues because they feel that the substantially greater yield—which could amount to several percentage points when measured against an AAA issue—is worth the extra risk. They point out that the evidence of default in corporates—like that of municipals—is very low. But these are very uncertain times. Disaster could strike. Look at Penn Central, W. T. Grant, Chrysler, the company that owns the Three-Mile Island nuclear generating plant, or Itel, the computer-leasing company. You ought to think twice about this approach if you want to sleep nights.

HOW TO BUY CORPORATE BONDS AND NOTES: Like Treasury securities, you can purchase corporate bonds either when they are issued or in the secondary market. In either case, the minimum denomination for corporate bonds is usually $1,000 and they are sold in multiples thereof.

The big advantage of buying a new issue is that you don't have to pay any commission or fee; the underwriters, the brokerage houses who are selling the new bonds, make their money on the difference between what they charge you for the issue and what they pay the issuing corporation. If you buy bonds that are already outstanding you do have to pay a fee, though it may not be as high as the commission you would pay on a stock purchase of the same dollar amount.

You have some broader choices as to yield, maturity, and even potential capital gains or losses when you purchase outstanding issues. If, for example, you buy a bond that is selling well below par, with the intention of holding it to maturity, you virtually guarantee yourself a capital gain. And the gain can be large and quick in this era of rapidly fluctuating interest rates. A one-percentage-point decline in long-term yields could boost the combined interest-plus-capital gain to 20% or more for a bond held for only a year; and yields have moved a lot faster than that recently.

You can often find many good-quality issues — A-rated or better — that hold out the hope of such gains, and those are the ones you should stick with. The prices of bonds issued by even the most solid of companies can decline, and even sharply, if interest rates generally have risen since the time of issue. (See the chapter on Fixed-Income Securities.) However, so-called deep-discount bonds — bonds that are selling substantially below their original issue price — tend to sell at lower yields than issues specifying interest rates closer to the going level; that's because the capital gains potential is large.

CHAPTER TWELVE

OTHER SHORT-TERM INVESTMENTS

FAIL-SAFE RATING ON . . .

Safety: These are sometimes of the highest order, close behind Treasuries.

Income: Some offer some of the highest yields
available on any low or even moderate-risk
investments.

Tax Status: Income is fully taxable at the Federal, state and local levels.

Whatever your overall investment strategy, whatever your particular investment needs, there will often be times when you will want to place at least some of your funds into very short-term vehicles—those cashable in a few days on up to a year. Indeed, some of these vehicles could do the job of rainy-day savings-account deposits. But there will be times when a considerable part of your investing also will be in the "short end of the market," rather than in long-term securities. This will be true, of course, whenever interest rates are rising steadily and you have reason to believe they will continue to do so for some time. You'll want to wait until long-term yields get to or close to peaks before lengthening out into notes or bonds.

Many of the short-term instruments that will be discussed in this chapter are the kind that require substantial amounts of cash and are usually bought and sold by large corporations and financial institutions and wealthy individuals; if you are a smaller-scale investor, you probably will not want to place your money directly into any of these instruments because the minimum required is too high or because buying them through a broker or a bank involves paying a fee. And, on a thirty- to ninety-day investment, even a $20 fee can result in a substantial reduction in your effective yield. Nevertheless, you should be aware of the opportunities because at some point you may have occasion to purchase one of these instruments directly and because there are ways of investing smaller amounts indirectly in these same money-market instruments.

Here is a rundown on some of these possibilities:

MONEY-MARKET MUTUAL FUNDS are the best and safest way for small investors to participate in the money market. A great many are using these funds these days as a place to park the short-term cash they would otherwise keep in a low-yielding passbook savings account or in a checking account or even in other short-term investments.

These mutual funds invest in Treasury bills, prime certificates of deposit, commercial paper, bankers acceptances, and other very short-term instruments. They pool the money of many individuals to achieve the kind of buying power that only a big institution can swing. One of their big attractions is the nearly instant liquidity they offer. You can usually get your money out overnight with a phone call or even by writing a check (usually for a minimum of $500). In addition, these funds provide investors with broad diversification, all the record-keeping, professional management, and low handling and brokerage charges.

The safety of principal varies a little from fund to fund, with most setting fairly high standards; they invest only in prime commercial paper — unsecured notes issued by corporations for relatively short periods — and only in certificates of deposit of banks of very large size, though this doesn't guarantee that they can't take a loss. But even those funds that will buy the CD's or commercial paper of less well-rated borrowers — to get a little better yield — can generally be considered fairly low in risk.

> When interest rates are rising, the yields these funds offer will generally trail the going market by a little, because they are always holding some instruments bought, say, several weeks previous at lower yields; the lags aren't great, though, because low-yielding paper soon runs off and is replaced with paper offering current rates. But the reverse situation obtains when interest rates start to fall. Then the yields remain higher a little longer. One more thing to keep in mind: At times, yields of different funds vary; on occasion, the spread can be as much as two points — so check out several before investing.

How to Buy—Almost every major mutual-fund organization offers a "no-load" money-market fund. Don't even consider a fund that charges a sales fee. Minimum investment is often as low as $1,000 to $2,000 and you can often add money in increments as small as $25 to $50 at a time.

The great appeal of money-market mutual funds and the increasing desire for tax-exempt income have spawned yet another short-term investment vehicle—the tax-exempt money-market mutual fund. It invests in short-term tax-exempt securities, and offers just about all the other features of the money funds, including checkwriting privileges in some cases. But this variant is not for everyone. Such funds yield substantially less than the straight funds; chances are that an individual would have to be in the top income-tax brackets to end up as well as in a taxable fund. So, before you invest in a tax-free fund, a little arithmetic is in order to see whether you will come out ahead.

Suppose you are in the 49% bracket with $100,000 to invest at a time when a straight money-market fund is yielding 12%. Your taxable income from the fund is $1,200—or $612 after Federal taxes. (It would be less, of course, if you were subject to state and maybe local income taxes, as well.) You would have to get more than 6.12% on your money to do better in a tax-free fund—a figure that could be adjusted downward to take account of state taxes.

LARGE CERTIFICATES OF DEPOSIT are receipts from a bank, savings bank, or savings and loan association for deposits of $100,000 or more which mature in a specified period of time and carry a specified interest rate. The banking authorities do not impose any limit on the interest rate financial institutions can pay on these "jumbo" CD's. (They do still continue to limit the rates on smaller CD's, those that were discussed in Chapter Six.) The large CD's issued by banks may be negotiable—that is, you can buy or sell one to another investor after it has been issued. But the large CD's of savings banks and savings and loans are not negotiable.

The CD's issued by the large banks in the money centers of New York, Chicago, and the West Coast are generally regarded as very safe investments. Those issued by smaller banks are at worst very slightly less so. And note that these certificates are insured—up to

$100,000—by the Federal Deposit Insurance Corp., just like any other deposit. CD's issued by big money-center banks usually yield at least a quarter to a half percentage point more than Treasury bills. But, during periods of tight money, when rates are rising generally, the spread can widen substantially, to well over a point.

How to Buy—You can buy a jumbo CD directly from a bank and pay no fee or you can purchase one in the secondary market through a bank or broker. But remember: The minimum is $100,000.

Some large brokerage houses also offer shares in funds that will invest your money in the CD's of large foreign banks; those CD's are not insured by the FDIC, of course, but they are considered quite safe because of the size and solidity of the issuing banks.

BANKERS ACCEPTANCES are usually chosen as investments by large financial institutions or by corporations. But, because they are sometimes bought by individuals in denominations as little as $25,000, they are included here for the sake of completeness. Essentially, they are like postdated checks, used to pay for goods—usually imports or exports. They carry a future date—maybe the day the goods are due to arrive. A bank "accepts" the paper by paying the seller of the goods—in effect, making a loan to the buyer; the seller, though, gets an amount reduced by the interest the bank charges. The bank can then sell the accepted check to an investor—again at a discount, though perhaps of a different amount—who gets the full amount on maturity, as he would on a Treasury bill.

Where to Buy: You can buy bankers acceptances through a bank or broker.
COMMERCIAL PAPER is also a vehicle largely of interest to big investors. As noted, it is simply an IOU issued by a corporation that needs short-term cash. These

IOU's are usually bought by other corporations which happen to be flush, although under certain circumstances they can be purchased by private investors.

Commercial paper is also rated as to quality, P-1 being the best grade on the most widely used scale, P-2 next, etc. It normally yields one-quarter to a full percentage point more than Treasury bills. During tight-money periods, however, that gap can widen substantially, along with the risk.

Where to Buy: You can buy commercial paper through brokers or occasionally directly from one of the large issuers, usually finance companies. Denominations can be as small as $5,000, although $25,000 is usually the minimum available; more typically, commercial paper sells in lots of $100,000 and more.

State and local governments meet temporary cash needs by offering short-term notes to investors. These are exempt from Federal income taxes—and often from state income taxes, as well. They were discussed in Chapter Ten—Tax-Exempt Securities.

SECTION III

SOME MORE RISK FOR MORE PROFIT

CHAPTER THIRTEEN

COMMON STOCKS

FAIL-SAFE RATING ON . . .

Safety: The certainty that money invested can be recovered intact is far less than is the case with debt obligations like bonds. Though the value of the stock of even the most solid corporation can zoom, it can also decline severely because of developments that can't always be foreseen.

Income: Dividends can fall far short of—or sometimes exceed—interest payments on fixed-income securities, depending on the over-all economy, monetary policy, the industry's prospects, the company's own fortunes, and its management's policies.

Tax Status: Each investor may exclude some dividend income from U.S. corporations; the balance of income is fully taxable, except for certain tax-free returns of capital—usually on utility stocks. Profits on sale of stock can sweeten the total return on an equity investment and may be eligible for the lower capital-gains tax rates.

Up to now, we have been focusing on ways to provide financial security and then to keep income as much ahead of inflation as we possibly can. Now comes a greater stress on making money — prudently . . . by Fail-Safe Investing, rather than speculating. And this means a heavy emphasis on common stocks — and real estate, too, as we'll see later on.

More successful investors have made more money in these two areas than in any others, including gold, silver, or diamonds. To be sure, that's not easy to document with the Dow-Jones Industrials Average during the Seventies; it rose a mere 21%. But the composite New York Stock Exchange Index did a lot better than that, rising 62%. And the American Stock Exchange was up a whopping 273% — 450% in the last six years of the past decade.

The fact that the AMEX issues did so well reflects in part the heavy concentration of its listing of companies in energy and high technology. Some of them were new firms with speculative overtones. But there were solid values, too — and on the Big Board as well.

Many of those who made it in stocks haven't done it with one fantastic winner, either, though a relative few did indeed end up with fortunes by getting into one spectacular growth issue early on. But even they had to stay with their holdings for years to reap the maximum returns; they didn't make quick killings by moving in and out in a few weeks or months. The fact is that, while there has been no perfect inflation hedge during this period, common stocks have outperformed savings accounts and certificates, good-quality notes and bonds, and just about every other income-earning investment except for real estate. But before considering the strategy that will probably work best for you, let's talk about some basic concepts, starting with the two kinds of stocks that corporations issue.

COMMON STOCKS are pure equity or ownership. They are held by the risk-takers who get the bulk of the profits when times are good and bear the brunt of the losses when things go the other way.

PREFERRED STOCKS reflect ownership, too. But they enjoy a prior claim on a fixed amount of dividends; in exchange for this "preferred" position, they usually (though not always) give up the right to any more of the profits than the fixed amounts. All other profits, if there are any, go to the holders of common stock. In a sense, preferreds are a hybrid—a cross between a bond and a common stock and ranking somewhere between the two in safety. Preferred stock is a favored method of financing by public-utilities companies.

> Note that preferred share-holders do not receive dividends if the company doesn't earn enough to pay them. In some cases, if the money isn't available, the shareholders are simply out of luck for that dividend period. In the case of so-called cumulative preferreds, arrears pile up and the unpaid dividends of past years must be cleaned up before common stock-owners can receive any payments. In general, if it is assured fixed-income that you are after, you might just as well stay with notes and bonds.

The common stocks of utilities have long been regarded as conservative investments and have behaved somewhat like bonds and preferreds. They are said to be interest-rate sensitive because the regulatory authorities in the state and Federal governments are supposed to set electric, gas, water, and telephone rates at levels assuring stockholders a "fair" return on their investment—in effect, something resembling a fixed return.

> Over the years, utilities commons have tended to move up or down in price with bonds or preferreds, going down in price when tight money raised yields, or up when money eased. Utilities, though, have one edge on bonds and preferreds: They can appreciate in price over

the long run as earnings are plowed back to increase the stockholders' capital—and, therefore, the amount of profit the authorities will allow. On the other hand, the profits of common stockholders are subject to certain restraints. Lately, for example, some utilities have had problems keeping up their earnings. The regulatory authorities haven't always authorized rate increases fast enough to offset the higher costs of oil and other fuels as well as other increases in operating expenses. And the authorities have been slow to let the companies make up for the losses from nuclear mishaps or shutdowns.

At this point, it may be worth stating a theme that you will find recurring over and over in the remaining chapters of this book: Once you move away from marketable fixed-income investments, where you have the rating agencies to guide you, it is essential to do extensive homework before investing—or to have it done for you.

Buying shares of ownership in a public corporation—common stocks—admits an investor to all the pleasures and drawbacks of ownership in any business. When times are good, the company's prospects are bright, and talented management makes the right decisions, the results can be very rewarding. But, for all the IBM's and Xeroxes, there are companies like Chrysler, too—a multibillion-dollar corporation whose only hope of staving off bankruptcy lay in huge government loan guarantees. Thousands of investors have seen its price plummet from a high of 72¾ in the past twenty years to a low near 4 in 1981.

Cases like Chrysler's come up relatively infrequently, to be sure. The risks involved in investing in stocks can be minimized—and the returns on investment increased—by choosing an effective investment strategy and employing some old and new techniques.

Buying mutual fund shares will enable you to avoid much of the homework involved in a do-it-yourself stock-buying program. And there is nothing wrong with this way of investing. In effect, you will be hiring professional managers at a reasonable cost. And you will benefit from the diversification that is difficult to achieve with less than, say, $25,000 to spread over four or five stocks. What's more, you can no doubt find a fund whose objectives jibe with yours.

There are five major kinds, with numerous variations.

• *Income funds*—They invest primarily in high-yielding stocks (and include bonds as well) for people who need a steady flow to live on.

• *Growth funds*—Your money is invested in companies in fast-growing fields, companies that usually pay small dividends while plowing back profits into future growth; here the goal is long-term capital gains—usually the objective of younger people trying to build up their assets.

• *Balanced funds*—These try to compromise, giving investors fair-sized dividends, but some growth potential, too, by investing in bonds and stocks.

• *Indexed funds*—On the theory that even most professionals can't do better than the market as a whole, these funds merely try to match its performance by investing in a portfolio designed to mirror one of the broad market indexes. Originally, these shares were available only to institutions, but at least one—in the Vanguard Group—now sells to individuals.

• *Special-situation funds*—These seek out new or unusually attractive situations in a special area, like oil, uranium, etc., where the gains may be spectacular if the chosen industry turns out to be a winner.

Mutual funds can also be classified according to the commission you pay—or don't pay. The older, traditional types, which can usually be bought through brokers, charge a one-time "load" of 3½% to 8% of your investment, depending on the particular fund and the amount you are investing; a good part of this goes to the sales agent. (A $5,000 purchase might involve an 8% charge; $100,000, 3½%.) But there are also "no-load" funds. These funds reach investors through frequent newspaper ads. The load funds insist that you will get what you pay for—that their performance over the years is superior to the no-loads. But many experts do not find any significant difference.

The record of the mutual funds is spotty, on the whole. Some small funds do spectacularly well for a few years, then falter. Success may reflect luck or skill in finding and staying with an explosive growth situation; once it peaks out, though, it is hard to find another and so performance may decline. There is also the fact that a fund's success attracts money, but there aren't always enough hot situations to absorb it; so the money goes into less spectacular performers, which is why many funds do little if any better than the stock market as a whole. Sometimes that's not bad, but at other times the performance is barely mediocre. Avoid funds run by one superstar—even one with a spectacular record for a year or two; he could make one mistake—with disastrous consequences—while a well-staffed fund could progress a little more slowly, but with steadier results. Investing in several funds, however, may reduce still further the danger that any one will have such a bad year that it seriously dents the over-all value of your investments.

Many investors probably couldn't do any better on their own. But some succeed all the time, and maybe you can. To do so, though, you must be willing to put in time and effort—and to enjoy the challenges or else you'll find it hard to keep a program going to the payoff point. Most of all, you'll need to have a clearly defined approach to stocks—a strategy.

> One dictionary defines the word strategy as "a plan, method or series of maneuvers for obtaining a specific goal or result." The term is used here to mean the process the investor pursues in reaching the decisions that, hopefully, will make him money; these are the rules that determine the timing and selection of the specific commitments he makes. Though many stock-market pundits believe that their own strategies are unique, they all tend to fall into a handful of broad categories—

and each category often involves key elements of another.

Many do-it-yourselfers don't follow any strategy at all. They merely "play the market," often buying on impulse on the basis of tips from friends or relatives, casual reading of the financial pages, or the advice of a brokerage-house salesman. Any new purchase has little relationship to the last, let alone to an overall plan.

If you are investing according to a plan, consciously or otherwise, it may reflect your own psychological makeup. (See Chapter Two.) Normally, it's the one with which you'll be most comfortable. But, it you aren't satisfied with the results, here are some others to consider:

Technical Analysis, or charting, sees the key to the timing of future share-price movements in past patterns of the over-all market's or of a particular stock's action. Technicians believe devoutly that the market's own behavior is the key to where it is going. They plot graphs showing dozens of statistical measures, each expert stressing those he thinks most important—price patterns, trend lines, moving averages, trading volume, volume of short sales. They painstakingly study esoteric concepts like "Dow divergence," "net field trend," and "climax indicator." It's a time-consuming process that takes great specialization. Some of this group consider "fundamental" factors like the state of the economy or an industry or a company's sales or profit prospects to be irrelevant to share-price performance; they insist that, at bottom, only the supply and demand for stocks—which in turn rest on greed and fear as key elements of human nature—determine market prices. Others don't deny that fundamental factors can be important for a stock's future price path. But they insist that technical analysis is best for pinpointing the timing of buy and sell moves. Technicians have had some spectacular successes, particularly in catching short-run market movements—but spectacular failures, too.

Picking the rapid-growth stocks of the fu-

ture—tomorrow's IBM's and Polaroids—can pay off big, of course. Such stocks tend to enjoy a superior product and management and be well positioned in a rapidly expanding field. Their inherent vigor can carry them unscathed even through recession periods. Lately, the high-technology and natural-resource groups have produced the most exciting performers. But stocks in these areas often make their most spectacular moves before the typical investor can get in. Share prices reach levels that run years ahead of earnings. At some point, companies that lack the products and the management needed to stay in the race begin to falter. So do the stocks' prices—too often before the small investor, who bought in near the highs, can get out. In other words, you have to be very right in picking the winners to make this strategy pay off.

Doing what the insiders do is attracting increasing attention from investors who reason that corporate directors and executives or major stockholders must know what the score is when they buy or sell their companies' stocks. Insiders are required by law to list their purchases and sales with the Securities and Exchange Commission, and those files are open for the public to see. Interesting trends are reported by major newspapers and several newsletters. Several studies have shown that insiders' transactions often do precede market price movements, up or down. It's not so much because the company people are acting on secret information—they can't, by law—but because they are in good position to judge the business's prospects. It sometimes takes as long as a year for insiders' judgments to be confirmed in share prices—and sometimes they prove wrong. One reason: Insiders often act for reasons unrelated to the companies' prospects—like when they need money for family purposes. Some market observers believe that an outsider can often arrive at the same conclusion indicated by investor trading just by studying the company's statistics, though that might take longer.

The Theory of Contrary Opinion—as applied to picking stocks—has proven quite successful for a number of investors in recent years. It calls for buying issues that are out of favor—stocks that, at the given time, don't have many followers. Those who swear by this approach believe that the market often errs in neglecting shares that are good, solid values. Why? Often because they don't happen to be "hot" or in fashion. As a result, the "contrarians" can take advantage of relatively low prices to get genuine bargains that in time will rise to their true-value levels. Such issues are sometimes those of companies that were in poor shape—or in depressed industries—but which are now positioned to do better. Their ratios of share prices to earnings are still low but will, in time, hopefully rise. The appreciation in railroad stocks not so long ago is reported to have yielded large capital gains to some contrarians.

Culling out the losers is a strategy that rests on the belief that avoiding stocks likely to drop in price will do more for an investor's over-all performance than concentrating on picking the winners. Studies have shown that weeding out stocks selling at above-average prices or yielding below-average dividends can pay off. Such issues tend to do more poorly than the market as a whole. More sophisticated analysis can often spot weaknesses, when these simpler measures do not. But this is an approach that isn't easy to apply. For every 100 buy recommendations that market professionals make, there are only about five sells.

Selling call-options on stocks you own and would choose for fairly long-term appreciation could give you a substantial return. It can stand as a strategy on its own or can, as we'll see, be integrated into the basic approach that's advocated below.

There are elements in several of these approaches that belong in a Fail-Safe Investing strategy—and some that don't. Technical analysis, for example, has little to contribute. It is much too complicated for the lay individual to deal with on his own; indeed, it's hard to find many nonprofessionals who have done well with such methods. It would be great to be able to pick the star growth stocks of the future, but there's a large speculative element in playing that game;

you could easily go wrong. And buying stocks just because they are out of favor runs a risk of ending up with some that deserve to be.

But you can pursue a low-risk and rewarding strategy for investing in common stocks by following these basic guidelines.

• *Invest for the long term.* Be patient. Don't expect to see—or take—profits for two years or more. There's one compensation: You don't have frequent sell decisions to make.

• *Sell out promptly, though,* if events disclose that you have made a mistake—that the company or its stock isn't behaving the way you expected it to.

• *Don't make your primary objective capital gains,* rather than income, because that could lead to taking risks that you don't mean to take. There is nothing inherently wrong about capital gains as a secondary objective, though.

• *Put 50% or more of your equity money into companies with established records of profitable growth,* even though they may be on brokers' "sell" lists. The gains in sales and profits don't have to match the rates of the glamor leaders; be satisfied with continuing growth of 10% a year. Look for companies with specialized products or services that can count on assured demand for years to come—pharmaceuticals and communications, rather than steel or auto parts.

> As 1981 began, a sample list of likely candidates would have included Sears and J. C. Penney among the beaten-down retailers. St. Regis and Domtar in paper. General Foods and Stop and Shop in foods. U.S. Gypsum and National Gypsum in building materials. Western Airlines and Emery Air Freight in transportation. But note that one year later a current list might be very different. A service like the Value Line Investment Survey would provide much of the statistical material you would need to make your own selections in accordance with the criteria set out above. (See Page 235.)

But you have to read the daily papers, company reports, and brokers' studies, as well.

• ***Don't make a commitment until you feel certain that you are making the right move.*** Limit yourself to only about five stocks; it would be hard to keep close tabs on many more.

• ***Don't overpay for the stock.*** Make sure that its price to earnings ratio is no more than, say, seven. If you have chosen correctly, the market will realize it in time and be willing to pay more for each dollar of earnings.

• ***Look for dividend yields of 6% or 7%.*** When the price-earnings ratios do go up, your total return—dividends plus capital gain—could easily reach 15% or even more.

• ***Don't ignore the likely leaders of the Eighties***—those in the defense and energy-natural resources groups. They warrant a significant part of the rest of your equity funds, because that's where so much of the economy's growth will center. Most are fairly fully priced, so try to buy them during one of the setbacks that constantly hit the market; a dip of 5% could be regarded as a trigger.

• ***But approach the new high-technology stocks with care.*** As already noted, many will fall by the wayside, and their price-earnings ratios will collapse. If you are inclined to take chances, limit your outlays for long shots to 5% or 10% of your stock portfolio. And, if you happen to get some of the initial offerings of hot new issues—Genetech and Apple Computer were recent examples—consider selling out immediately; in many cases, the stocks will never be as high again as the levels reached during the first days' run-ups.

• ***Whenever possible, choose stocks that are eligible for trading in the options market.*** There is a good reason why you may want your stocks to be eligible for options trading. You would have the opportunity to capitalize on a rapidly expanding technique that can sharply increase the return you may reap on essentially conservative stocks. The method involves selling certain options.

> To recap briefly first, the options market began in 1973, and participation and volume have been growing rapidly ever since. Options are now being traded on a growing number of exchanges.

In essence, a securities option offers the right to buy or sell 100 shares of any of a large number of widely held common stocks. An option-holder may exercise his option within a certain period of time, and he can only exercise it at a specified price. Options can be traded—bought and sold—like the stock that underlies them; their value will fluctuate with that of the underlying shares, though not always in a fixed relationship.

There are two types of options available:
The "put" option gives the buyer the right to sell a stock at a given price. He pays a premium for that right and, in effect, is betting that the market will go down below the specified price. If he is right, he can exercise the option, and pocket the difference between the specified price and the market quotation at the time the transaction is closed out. (He has certain commission costs, too, which have to be deducted to determine his net profit.)
The "call" option gives the buyer the right to buy a stock at a given price. He, in effect, is betting that the price will go up and give him his profit. Either kind of option involves contract maturities originally set for three, six, or nine months, always maturing on the third Friday of the month.
Either way, the buyer hopes to take advantage of the leverage provided—leverage he wouldn't have if he bought the stock outright or which would be relatively small if he purchased it with 50% down, which has been the minimum the government required for much of the recent past. Be-

fore getting down to the recommended way to use options, let's see how they work:

> Suppose you buy a call on the XYZ Co.—the right to buy 100 shares at a so-called strike price of 50 on January 15—several months hence. The stock is selling for 47 and the market price of the option is 3 ⅛—that is, you pay a premium of this much to the seller of the option. You also pay a commission to the broker that's subject to variation, but could be around $80. Total investment: $392.50—that is, $312.50 plus $80.

Now, if the stock goes to 60, the option price would also rise by, say, around $8 a share, to 11. The buyer can wait until January 15 and exercise his option, take the stock, sell it—and realize his gross profit of ten points or $1,000. More likely, though, he will just sell the option to avoid another stock commission for net proceeds—after commissions—of more than $500, and a net profit of more than 100%.

> Contrast this with the return on a straight purchase of the underlying stock. The 100 shares of XYZ would cost him $4,700 plus a commission of $80—$4,780 in all. Selling at 60, with the same commission, would mean proceeds of $5,920 for a net profit of $1,140. On his investment of $4,780, that's a return of 24%.

This is not to urge buying call options—or puts for that matter, either. Essentially, either approach is gambling—gambling that your assessment of the outlook for the particular stock is good. If it is, you'll make a bundle; if it isn't, you lose your premium—all of it, or only a part if you decide to buy it back before the option expires (assuming it still has some value). Neither way can be deemed Fail-Safe Investing.

Now let's focus on how options can boost the return on stocks in a relatively conservative way.

***The method involves selling call options,
not buying them.*** You buy a stock that you like and
would feel comfortable owning for, say, six months, a year
or even longer—a stock that you can afford to sit with even
it if goes down for a while. You get the premium, less commission, and you add it to your dividends, plus the difference between what you paid and the strike price if the stock
should be called away from you.

Let's say you bought 100 shares of XYZ Co. at 47 ($80 in
commissions) because it seems fairly priced, pays 7% a year
in dividends and is one of the better stocks in an industry
that should do even better next year. If the stock just sits or
fails to top 50, it won't be called away from you. So you keep
the premium of 3⅛ which, less commission, nets you
$232.50 for four months—or at an annual rate of earnings of
$697.50. Add that to your 7%—$329—annual dividend and
you have made a $1,026.50-a-year return on your money—
or more than 21%.

Now—suppose the stock goes up and is called away. You
add the $3 capital gain—the difference between what you
paid and the strike price—to get an overall, annualized total of $1,326.50 in dividend, option premium and capital
gain combined. After the commission involved on the delivery, your return on investment would be about 26%
($1,246.50÷$4,780).

You won't always get that good a combination of divi-
dent, premium, or capital gain. But returns of 15% or 18%
are quite common. As noted, though, you have to be comfortable with the stock in the first place. And you have to
reconcile yourself to only modest, limited capital gains
should the stock go up. The option-buyer—the gambler—
will reap the big profit should the stock's price zoom.

> Your strategy of buying an out-of-favor stock and hold-
> ing it until the market recognizes its inherent worth
> may have to be suspended when you are selling op-
> tions. But the good returns from an option transaction

will give you that much more to put into another issue
that meets the strategy's guidelines.

You'll notice that some investors' favorite ploys have not
been mentioned in connection with the basic strategy of
stock selection — dollar-averaging, convertible bonds and
preferreds, closed-end investment companies, buying on
margin, selling short. They have all produced good results
for some individuals at certain times. But the catalogue of
such possibilities can be endless. In the long run, concentration on solid, undervalued stocks and those in the areas likely to grow fastest in the Eighties seems to promise the best
results with the least risk.

CHAPTER FOURTEEN

REAL ESTATE

FAIL-SAFE RATING ON . . .

Safety: Some real-estate investments compare favorably with, say, corporate bonds while others are a crap-shoot. Much depends on the nature of the property chosen and the way it is financed.

Income: It can be very high or nil, varying with the kind of property.

Tax status: Often extremely favorable.

There is no area of investing that is as varied or complex — or as potentially rewarding — as real estate. The possibilities and ramifications are almost infinite. Not only are there many kinds of properties but, within each category, almost every deal has its unique features that have to be studied and allowed for. Weighty tomes have been written on specific aspects of real estate — selecting, appraising, financing, taxation, etc.

So this chapter can hardly be anything more than an introduction that highlights only some basic principles — principles, though, that have made many individuals far wealthier than they would be now from just about any other kind of investment, even including stocks. Specifically, we will discuss four broad areas: your primary residence, a second or vacation home, income-producing property, and vacant land.

But first let's list some basic rules that apply to all real-estate investments, regardless of kind.

- **Be prepared to devote considerable time** to studying the property, the area in which it is located, and comparable values. As stressed in the case of stocks, don't make a commitment until you feel that you know what you are doing.
- **Hire a local expert,** or appraiser, to give you a second independent judgment to back up your own. He'll be worth the fee. Your lawyer, accountant, or banker can give you the name of a reliable professional.
- **Shop for financing.** Some lenders will give you more at a lower interest rate than others — especially a bank, savings bank, or savings and loan association where you have been an established customer.
- **Don't let greed lure you into overextending** — into mortgaging everything to the hilt (including your home) so that you are vulnerable to a break in the market or an error in your judgment. Even in a climate of generally rising real-estate val-

ues, some regions or types may suffer severe, if at times only temporary, setbacks.

- ***Don't be reluctant to offer less*** —maybe even thousands less—than the seller is asking. You never can tell how much he has padded the price to give him bargaining leeway. Or he may have trouble finding a buyer who can arrange the financing. And if the seller stands firm, you can always go higher.

- ***There is something to be said for dealing with an agent you can trust,*** one who specializes in the kind of property you are seeking. First of all, the seller usually pays the commission. Even if you are the seller, the commission may be worthwhile because the agent may keep you from asking too little—or too much—and help arrange financing. Of course, if you can do your own selling, you can save the commission of 6% or so on residential property, maybe 10% on commercial.

Now—let's look at specific kinds of real-estate investments.

YOUR PRIMARY RESIDENCE

At this point, the very first question that arises is: Should you own your own home at all? Or would you be better off renting? There are three aspects to consider.

Not the least is your personal preference. Are you the kind who likes to putter and do his own maintenance—or do you like someone else to do it for you? Do you want the security of sinking roots in a community—or would you rather be free to pick up and move, without having become involved with neighbors?

Can you swing the down payment and the other up-front costs that home-ownership entails? Veterans can get by with little if anything down, and mortgages insured by the Federal Housing Administration only require relatively small down payments; but even these are often hard to arrange. Private mortgage insurance can reduce the size of a down payment at a fairly reasonable premium cost. Nevertheless, a conventional mortgage could easily call for a 20% down payment

Finally, is your own home a good deal from a financial point of view—that is, as an investment? Usually, it is—at least, it you will be owning for a minimum of two or three years and get your up-front costs behind you. Indeed, for the typical American family, its home has been the best—often the only—possible hedge against inflation. But you ought to do your own arithmetic to see the advantages for yourself. This involves figuring it both ways.

>   *The calculation on renting is quite simple:* What do you pay each month, plus—if your lease says you have to pay for them—utilities and maintenance costs like painting.

>   *In the owning calculation, you want to include,* as a cost, the interest you forego on the money you put into the down payment, plus a factor for depreciation of the heating system and appliances (which, as a homeowner, you can't deduct for tax purposes), as well as taxes, mortgage interest, maintenance and repair costs, and the settlement costs, which must be spread out over the life of the mortgage.

At first glance, renting seems to be far and away the best way to go. But the shrinking supply of rental units—relative to demand, at any rate—suggests that rents could be rising rapidly in years ahead, especially if rent controls are removed. What's more, the owner has two advantages which the renter does not share. One is the fact that the tax laws strongly favor the homeowner; he can deduct his interest payments and real-estate taxes. The second is that inflation could still keep increasing the value of your home, offsetting the depreciation from the modest wear-and-tear that comes with a structure's age. The home appears to be the one asset that appreciates in value as it is used. On the whole, homes certainly outperformed stocks and bonds in the decade of the Seventies.

And, as noted in Chapter Four, there is no certainty that the rate of inflation will subside significantly in, say, the first half of the 1980s. It could—but prudence argues against betting that way. And, even in a recession, the worst that is likely to happen to a well-selected house bought at a fair market price is that its value will level off temporarily, or only decline a little. And, before long, the rise in its value will probably resume. That has been the history of the business cycles of the past four decades.

Once you have decided to own, do you buy an existing house or build your own? Here, the calculations may be more evenly balanced. In building, you get a home that's much closer to your dream—and it's new, with less worry about hidden faults. But if you buy an existing house, you see exactly what it is—what it looks like—and you don't have to deal with architects, builders, and the inevitable cost overruns; on the other hand, you might have to pay for considerable fixing up. In many cases, though, you may get more for your money in an existing home.

The best time to buy is in the off-season, when relatively few people are looking for homes. In the North and West, that could be mid-November to late February, when the weather is cold and nasty; in some of the warmer areas of the Sun Belt, the best time to house-hunt could be the summer. There is also something to be said for being an early bird in a new apartment building or subdivision. As projects begin to sell out, builders tend to raise prices on their dwindling inventory.

After you have found a well-priced home, there is still the problem of financing—a difficult one these days that isn't likely to get easier until inflation subsides significantly. Even if high interest rates scare away many would-be buyers, mortgage money will no doubt remain hard to come by. Where lenders are willing to make loans, the chances are that they will only offer one or more of the three new types that are just coming into wide use—mortgages that will increase yields to the lenders at the same time that rates they pay to savers are going up.

The Renegotiable Rate Mortgage (RRM) is sometimes called the rollover mortgage. By its terms, the interest rate would be renegotiated every three to five years. The rate can rise or fall by a maximum of a full percentage point for each year, in line with an officially published index. The total increase or decrease that can occur over the life of the mortgage is 5 percentage points, though lenders may be given even more leeway to raise rates. One draw-back from the buyer's point of view is the fact that he doesn't know just what he'll be paying later on; on the other hand, borrowers won't be locked in at record or near-record rates if they should happen to finance during a tight-money period. And they do have ninety days to shop around for a better deal at the end of each renewal period, though the lender must renew, if asked.

The Variable Rate Mortgage (VRM) is somewhat like the RRM, but it has no intermediate renewal date; rather—under recent rule changes by the regulatory agencies—the interest rate can be raised or lowered a percentage point quarterly or semi-annually or even every month in line with a government index. Increases can total 5 points over the mortgage's life, but there is no limit to the decreases. This kind of loan is expected to become the most popular.

The Graduated Payment Mortgage (GPM) provides for lower monthly payments to start with than under a conventional loan, then a gradual rise in the amount for five or ten years; after that, the payments level off—but at a higher amount than a flat fixed-rate loan would specify. Overall, the cumulative interest paid is greater than would be the case for a standard-type loan. But the GPM is designed for young home-buyers—generally those with government-insured mortgages—whose incomes will rise as they grow older.

Down payments could still be 20% or more for users of the new mortgages (except perhaps in the case of GPM). For some families, that's quite steep, especially with the average home price heading toward $75,000 and higher. It could also be high for investors like yourself. Many want as much leverage as they can arrange to get the most profit on the least amount of their capital—even on their own homes. In effect, they would like to use as much of other people's money as possible to finance their purchases, keeping most of the future capital gains for themselves while repaying the loans in dollars worth less than when they were borrowed.

How do you leverage when mortgage money is tight and/or down payments seem too steep? Enter "creative financing"—the key to making many an impossible deal go through. In essence, the term covers just about any method or scheme that substitutes ingenuity and a lick or a promise for the hard cash that the buyer can't or won't put up. The possibilities are limited only by the human imagination. They range well beyond such prosaic standbys as Veterans Administration or Federal Housing Administration no- or low-down–payment loans or borrowing from relatives or on a car. The most commonly used and most serviceable of more recent techniques are these:

Assuming an existing mortgage sidesteps the entire question of getting a new loan—if the present lender will permit it. He must, if it's a VA or FHA loan or one originally made by state-chartered institutions in certain states. Even where they have the right to refuse, some lenders will agree to takeover for a fee or a moderate increase in the old mortgage's rate.

Getting the seller to take back a second mortgage can bridge the gap between the loan that a bank or savings institution will make and the down payment the buyer can afford. Terms are negotiable, depending on how badly the seller wants to sell or the buyer wants to buy. The interest rate can range from the going rate for first mortgages to the full 20% and more that seconds have commanded. Length of the loan can be as little as a year—or as much as five. Monthly amortization can be high—or so little that the buyer must repay virtually all of the original principal when the second mortgage comes due.

Placing a second mortgage with an investor, where the seller can't afford to hold it, can work just as well. The interest rate on the note may be low, as a result of the buyer's tough bargaining, but the seller can discount it, often through the real-estate broker handling the sale; the investor gets it at less than face value for a rich yield on the money he actually puts up.

Arranging a "wrap-around" mortgage can make a home purchase go where there's an existing low-interest loan, which the original lender may not permit the buyer to assume. So the property stays in the seller's name; the buyer gets a "deed by contract" and makes all his payments to the seller—on the first mortgage as well as the second that's involved. The seller then makes the payments to the first-mortgage holder. Where a mortgage can't be assumed, the contract may be the only evidence of the sale; it needn't be recorded and, hence, doesn't give the first-mortgage holder the right to call the loan.

Leasing with an option to buy permits both buyer and seller to make a deal but put off the transfer of title—and the permanent financing—for a year or two or some other agreed-upon date until credit conditions improve. The buyer's down payment is an "option to buy." Meanwhile, he pays rent which can be applied to reduce the purchase price.

Leasing land for, say, forty-nine or even ninety-nine years can trim the purchase price, the down payment, and the monthly carrying charges to the point where a home becomes affordable. Indeed, homes in Hawaii have been sold with land leases since foreigners first came to the islands. It's a widespread practice in England, too. Land rent goes up every several years. Some deals give the buyer an option to purchase the land after the first few years.

Note the provision of the 1978 tax law that will give many homeowners a big once-in-a-lifetime break when they sell their primary residences. Owners over fifty-five, who have lived in their homes for three of the last five years before a sale, can escape capital-gains tax on the first $100,000 of profit. And there is still the long-standing provision that exempts the profits made by anyone on a sale from capital-gains taxation if they are reinvested in another primary residence within eighteen months.

INCOME-PRODUCING PROPERTY

Weighing risk against return, few investments can offer the potential of carefully selected income-producing real estate. But never forget that your investment is illiquid; you couldn't sell out with anything like the speed that you could with stocks and bonds. And there is also a vast potential for error—and loss, especially in this era of prices that are already so high. Knowing what you're doing is the key.

Finding good properties at a viable price has been difficult recently in several parts of the country. Foreigners, especially the oil-producers, are loaded with dollars and have been in position to outbid domestic investors for the big projects. There has also been intense competition for medium-sized and smaller properties. It can slacken some, during tight-money periods such as began in the fall of 1979—periods in which a shrinkage in the supply of mortgage money keeps investors out of the market. But, when credit conditions ease, the hunt intensifies again.

A new investor, therefore, would do best beginning with the purchase of a single-family home for rental, though the principles would be the same for vacation home or office building. Such a property is easier to investigate and evaluate, especially if the buyer focuses on his own or nearby neighborhoods. He should choose properties that he can personally check at any time; being an absentee landlord can be an invitation to trouble. A single-family home would also be relatively easier to finance.

Suburban properties are most popular with beginning real-estate investors. But there may be more profit—and certainly more challenge as well as risk—

in properties in poorer neighborhoods. You don't want to go into an area that's going to stay a slum forever, and catching a reviving area before prices have appreciated isn't easy. But a seedy slum can quickly become chic enough to attract young singles or families. Study and imagination can really pay off on this sort of deal.

And the growing shortage of rental units reduces the need to worry about getting tenants for attractive houses or apartments; it further underlies the possibilities for tax-sheltered income for retirees and others.

How does a buyer determine the right price for a property? The first step is to see the prices at which recent sales have gone by checking county records. This is tiresome, but it helps in arriving at current values for comparable properties. In the end, the price should also reflect such factors as the availability of properties generally, the longer-term trend of prices and values in the area, the cost and availability of mortgage money, and the negotiating skills of both parties. Constant surveying of the market should make a perceptive buyer confident of his judgment as to value. But if he still has doubts, or wants to be extra sure, he should call in an expert; his bank can no doubt suggest some names.

Getting an engineer or licensed house-inspection service to check an older property is a "must" step to be taken before signing a contract. (They are listed in the Yellow Pages under "Building Inspection Service.") The inspector should look at such construction basics as the roof, the condition of the heating and air conditioning systems, and the status of the bathrooms and the kitchen with its appliances. Ask them to estimate the costs of getting the house into shape—and keeping it that way.

Assuming the price and the property's condition pass muster, the next step is to look at the deal's arithmetic. It could be very sweet. The essentials are the same for a big project as well as a single-family home. Here's a relatively simple example:

Assume that an investor buys an $80,000 house with a 20% down payment and a 12% mortgage for the rest. A rental of $600 a month—three quarters of 1% of the home's price—would be reasonable; that's $7,200 a year. Monthly expenses might run $795—$640 in interest, $80 in taxes, and $75 for repairs and insurance. Include, say, $50 a month for payment on principal and the investor seems to be paying out $845 a month or $10,140 annually and losing $2,940 a year.

But many investors are prepared for this sort of "loss." Their sights are fixed on the tax shelter their investment gives them, and even more importantly on the prospects for long-term appreciation in the value of the property. (And note that the $50 a month in amortization is being added to equity; it is not a cost, meaning that the $2,940 loss is really only $2,340.)

Looking at the shelter, those expenses—$795 a month × 12, or $9,540—are deductible costs. In addition, the investor can deduct as depreciation a portion of the purchase price that is allocatable to the cost of the building—5½% for each full year under the President Reagan tax program. (You can't depreciate land.) If the building is worth $64,000, then $3,520 can be taken in depreciation. Adding this to the $9,540 means a total of $13,060 in deductions. Subtracting the income of $7,200, that leaves a loss of $5,860 for tax purposes.

For the married investor in the 37% bracket, that's a Federal tax saving of $2,168. Subtracting from the $2,340 loss, he is out-of-pocket $172 the first year. And this points up the fact that an investor usually has to be in the highest brackets to show a positive cash flow.

Now suppose, though, that the property appreciates only 5% a year in value—which would be far below the rate of recent years and below the pace that many see for years to come. That's $4,000 a year, or a 25% return before capital-gains taxes on the $16,000 investment. Even if you deduct the $172 loss, the "yield" is almost 24%. And if the property increases 10% in value, the rate of return would be about

49%. Even after taxes and the selling commissions that would be incurred on disposal, it would still be very high.

So far, we have been assuming that the property will be in the same shape when you sell it as when you first bought it. But quite a few investors have found that they can increase the profit on a deal substantially by the use of a little imagination. A fresh coat of paint or some new shutters can do wonders for the appearance and the price you get for a drab or rundown but otherwise sound property.

> For investors in higher brackets, the tax advantages — and the yields — will be that much higher.

There are two variations of the single-family home deal that quite a few small investors have found rewarding:

One is the condominium. In some cities in recent years, as many as 20% of all newly completed condos were purchased for investment — for rental pending sale at a capital gain. And, with the rental market strong, these units have been easy to fill at viable rents. Indeed, some owners have resold units after a year or two, realizing perhaps twice the cash they put in; then they used the money to pyramid — that is, to buy two new units — then four, etc.

But nothing is guaranteed; it's important to keep that in mind. Things can go wrong; even though the probabilities may be relatively minor, they do exist. What happens if the market softens and the condos are hard to keep rented? The mortgage payments must continue. And what happens if the owner is forced to bail out at a time when others in the same boat decide to do so, too? Sales may have to go at distress prices that wipe out profits and maybe even part or all of original equity.

> (Condominiums are not the same as the cooperatives that are permitted under the laws of a relatively few states. A condo confers ownership of a unit in a project, plus an interest in common features such as land, basement, halls, and stairs; each owner takes out his own

mortgage. In a cooperative, you own stock in a nonprofit corporation that gives you a "proprietary lease" to occupy certain space, with the mortgage covering the entire building. You have only your stock in the co-op to sell. This could mean that you may be restricted in selling out by rules that give the co-op the right to approve your buyer.)

The second variation is rehabilitation of rundown properties that can often be bought at bargain prices. A number of investors have made fortunes pursuing this strategy with single-family homes and small apartment buildings—and have made additional fortunes writing books about it. But it is critically important to estimate accurately the costs of getting the property into shape. A buyer who can do much of the repair work himself can substantially increase the profits he can make. The creative financing methods available to purchasers of personal homes can also be used by investors in income property.

But don't let a high mortgage rate scare you away from an otherwise attractive proposition. If the arithmetic works in your favor even at 14% or 15%, go ahead. Just make sure that you have the right to pay off the mortgage in advance when financing conditions ease, with little or no penalty. That way you can refinance the property and increase your yield even further. Of course, if the high rates make the deal unworkable—as they very well might—hold off until the mortgage market improves, even though you may have to pass up a particular property.

Note that, as an investor in business property, you won't be able to take advantage of the $100,000 once-in-a-lifetime exclusion that Congress has granted on profits from the sale of a primary residence by those over fifty-five. There are, however, some tax arrangements that do let investors defer the tax on real-estate profits.

One is the installment sale. Under present law, if you spread the proceeds of a sale over several years, you can prorate the profits over the period during which the payments are received. This avoids the bunching of income that could push you into a very high bracket and increase the total in taxes that you would pay.

Exchanging property is a more ambitious way to defer taxes on real-estate profits. The law permits tax-free exchanges for property "of like kind" — vacant land swapped for an office building, for example. Thus, someone with a built-up equity in investment property that he originally bought cheap can trade it for an income-earning asset of similar value that may yield substantial tax benefits — and he won't have to pay tax. Property exchanges are a lot more complicated than they seem and call for expert counsel.

A VACATION HOME

Owning a second home in a resort area, one that you can rent out, can give you the advantages of an investment that are enumerated above, plus some pleasure for you. But the tax law that Congress enacted in 1976 severely restricts your personal use — that is, if you still want to reap the maximum investment benefit. In other words, if you want the investment advantages, you have to treat the vacation home primarily as a business enterprise.

You'll lose major tax benefits if you use your vacation home more than fourteen days a year or more than 10% of the number of days it is used for rental plus personal purposes — whichever is greater. Those benefits include deductions for depreciation, utilities, maintenance and repair, insurance, and other costs that a homeowner cannot usually deduct for his primary residence.

> And there are certain other limitations besides: You have to reduce the amount of expenses you deduct by the proportion of the time you used the house to the total time it is occupied. Rental to family members, even at fair rent, counts as personal use.

Don't be quick to go into any of the time-sharing propositions that have grown so popular in recent years. They are certainly not a good investment. And they may be no great bargains as vacation retreats, either.

To be sure, you can buy a piece of a beachfront apartment, ski chalet, or resort cottage in Florida, Sun Valley, or almost any vacation area with a relatively small amount of cash. You, as one of five to fifty partners, will own your proportionate share of the unit for something between $2,000 and $12,000. The average price in this country is close to $4,000 for a one-week slot, plus about $120 a year for maintenance—and the purchase can often be financed. Some 200,000 buyers have gone this route with the number climbing every year since 1977. The lures: assurance of a nice place to go, plus the deductions for your share of the taxes and interest.

But there are potential drawbacks. Though the cost of an individual slice is small in number of dollars, you and your other partners would probably be paying an inflated price for the unit. You might not be able to recoup your money on resale—if you can find a buyer. What's more, the annual costs can be steep; you must reckon in the income you forego on the cash you put up—say, 13% on $4,000 or $520 a year in the case of an average-priced unit— plus maintenance and then all your normal vacation costs of plane fare, food, and so on. And what if you later decide that you don't like the place all that much, or that you don't want to come back every year? You can't be sure that a swap can be arranged for you. Finally, there have been cases of mismanagement that have wiped out the buyers' money. Run this sort of deal by your lawyer or accountant, too.

VACANT LAND

The belief that land is the safest possible investment is deeply imbedded in the thinking of many investors, active and potential. Didn't Will Rogers say: "Buy land—they ain't making any more of the stuff"? But, in actual fact, land can be a very risky speculation. By no stretch can it be called Fail-Safe Investing.

You simply can't be sure that all land is certain to increase in value. There are millions of acres in this country that are worth very little today—and may still have little value 10 or 20 or 100 years from now. To be sure, it's also true that big profits have been made in land and will be again. Demand for good, well-located property will continue to expand as farmers add to holdings for greater efficiency, foreigners invest their dollars, and the growing population needs homes. Meanwhile, the supply keeps shrinking as more and more acreage is developed into industrial sites, shopping centers, airports, roads, and housing.

As with any kind of real estate, the key is making the right selection and arranging the right financing. In delving further into the subject, let's break it into two parts—buying larger tracts of, say, 50 or 100 acres or more and buying lots of 5 or 2 acres or even less.

First—the larger tracts. Obviously, if you are fortunate enough to buy in the right place at the right time for the right price, you could realize many times your investment. But just buying land near a big city, then sitting back to let urban growth make you rich, is playing the long shots. You may discover that the expected development is taking place on the other side of town—or even in another town.

Even buying good farm land is no guarantee that you'll come out ahead. Experts say that farm land has gone up so fast, and is now so high, that it can't pay off unless it is slated for development as a housing project, industrial site, shopping center, or the like. If it isn't, you are stuck with property that can be leased for a relatively modest rental, but probably not enough to cover your land-loan payments and taxes and still yield a profit. After all, you can take no depreciation on undeveloped land.

Some successful land investors concentrate on parcels that have already appreciated some because the trend of growth and development already indicates that its time is not too far away. They'll pay a fairly substantial price, though with a relatively small down payment. Even a 25%

or 50% increase over several years can pay off in a handsome profit computed on the relatively limited amount of equity involved. But this would have to be considered a conservative land operation—conservative as these things go.

Some points to consider in buying tracts of land:

Bone up on the area you are considering, the watchword for all real-estate investment—and all other investing, too. Check out every aspect of the area—its zoning prospects, etc. Buy only if you are reasonably certain development is on the way.

Recognize the risks you run, if your judgment should prove wrong.

Don't be lured by low down payments and modest carrying costs. Leverage—using borrowed money—cuts both ways. If you are stuck with a big mortgage, those interest charges can eat you alive.

Invest only cash that you don't expect to need for a long period of time—and, even then, put only a minor part of your assets into land. Be prepared for a long wait until a payoff.

Be especially wary of foreign land. It's hard to keep up with the laws and regulations of other countries; most likely, you can't fully appreciate the pitfalls you may fall into and perhaps the obligations that you may be assuming.

Now—turning to smaller lots: People spent an estimated $4 billion during 1978 for undeveloped lots. Some plan to build vacation or retirement homes or to use the property for campsites. But others hope to resell at a profit.

Many of these buyers, though, will find that they're stuck with worthless parcels. Despite Federal and state efforts to police the business, some unscrupulous operators are still selling desert land lacking water for fancy prices (see Chapter Twenty). One reason they get away with it is that buyers don't—or can't—look at what they're buying beforehand.

Many other sellers are reputable, to be sure. They deliver what they promise—homesites in viable communities.

Those whose projects involve more than fifty lots to be sold in interstate commerce must register their developments with the Office of Interstate Land Sales Registration of the Federal Department of Housing and Urban Development. Before they can accept an order they must provide the prospective purchaser with a Property Report detailing information about the development.

Buyers simply have to be careful. There are few likelier ways to lose money than indiscriminate buying of lots—especially those in remote areas. Isolation makes development difficult, it not impossible. Yet, without the prospect of development, those lots cannot appreciate in value.

So, read the Property Report closely before you sign a contract. You'll have no one to blame but yourself if you ignore disclosures of a project's drawbacks.

Ask the salesman to enumerate in writing the essential services that will be provided such as sewers, water supplies, and garbage disposal; about the utilities in place or contracted for; about your taxes and other obligations; about who pays for and maintains the roads; about when the community center and swimming pool will be built—and how much it will cost you to use them. Ask for the names of people who have already settled in the project—and check them out.

Avoid a hasty decision: Resist high-pressure sales efforts which can gloss over the defects listed in the Property Report. Don't be influenced by free dinners, gifts, etc.

Check the contract with a lawyer experienced in real estate before you sign. Get him a sample copy of the deed.

In the end, don't buy a small lot in a vacation or retirement area unless you feel that you are going to use it yourself. Chances are it will make a poor investment.

CHAPTER FIFTEEN

REAL-ESTATE SECURITIES

FAIL-SAFE RATING ON . . .

Safety: They can be as safe—or as risky—as real estate itself.

Income: Yields can be as high, too.

Tax status: In most cases, not as favorable as property itself.

Many investors will find buying or owning real property unsuited to their needs. It may require more time and judgment than they feel they can provide—or they may not have sufficient cash to swing a viable but expensive property. For these, there are several kinds of easily purchased real-estate securities that offer benefits that are almost as substantial as outright ownership and are, therefore, very much worth considering.

Such securities can, for example, provide professional expertise in the selection and management of good properties. And the minimum amount you can invest could, in some cases, be quite small. On the other hand, those who are, in effect, doing the spadework for you expect to be compensated to an extent that might seem quite generous, which means that there will be somewhat less for you.

There are two other aspects of real-estate securities that a potential investor should keep very much in mind. One is the fact that, with some exceptions, real-estate securities—like direct investments in property—are illiquid; your interest can't always be easily sold, and you may be locked in long past the time that you'd like to get your money out. The second caveat: As in all investments, risk is related to return; the greater the potential yield, the more danger of a loss of principal. So think carefully before you put a significant part of your capital into such assets.

Now—for a rundown on the various securities you can buy.

FIRST MORTGAGES

These are the least risky of the paper forms of profiting from real estate. They are loans backed by real property, commercial and industrial as well as residential. Should the owner-borrower fail to pay interest and/or principal as it is due, the mortgage-holder can foreclose and take over the property. If the underlying property represents good value, if the mortgage total is substantially less than the worth of the property, and if the borrower is financially solid and able to meet his payments, a mortgage can be a superior investment. Yields can exceed those of corporate bonds, and amortization payments provide a flow of cash for new investment. But a mortgage-holder does not enjoy the tax-shelter benefits of owning property outright—no depreciation, no write-offs for taxes, etc. In other words, the mortgage is more like a bond—with an amortizing feature—than a true real-estate venture. And foreclosure can be a costly, messy business should taking over the property become necessary. So it's important to be selective about the borrower as well as the property.

First-mortgage loans are usually made and held by financial institutions—banks, savings and loan associations, insurance companies, and pension funds. Government agencies that buy mortgages to support the housing market own huge amounts as well. Individuals own some, too, but the minimums involved these days for even a condominium apartment—up to $40,000 or $50,000—are more than most individual investors care to commit to a single venture.

SECOND MORTGAGES

These have long played a greater role in individual investors' plans than firsts. In recent years, though, even large commercial banks have joined finance companies, credit unions, and other moneylenders in making second mortgages on the equity in private homes. The rise in home values brought on by inflation, but also by the growth of many areas, has provided larger equity bases for residential second mortgages than previously was the case.

> In addition to the traditional function of providing the difference between what a first-mortgage lender is willing to advance and the down payment a buyer can raise, second mortgages more recently have been used by homeowners to finance college, a business, or even a grand vacation.

A second mortgage, of course, resembles a first in that it is a loan against the property. But it is second in line behind the first. Thus, it is a riskier proposition than a first mortgage. If the owner fails to meet his payments, the holder of the second mortgage can foreclose. But if he has to buy it himself at the auction that may be legally required to avoid letting the property go for far less than it is worth, he's stuck with it and must himself make the first-mortgage payments; if he doesn't, he is subject to foreclosure himself and will get some of his investment back only if a sale brings more than the first-mortgage owner is owed.

In past years, 14% or 15% returns on second mortgages made for three to ten years were fairly common; the principal amounts were often as low as $5,000 to $10,000. But loans up to $25,000—and more—have lately been made fairly frequently, and interest rates have topped 20%. In states with relatively low usury ceilings, loans for "business purposes" are often exempt—and second-mortgage loans are sometimes termed that by the borrowers.

Many investors have shied away from second mortgages because of the possible risks. They have assumed—all too often correctly—that a buyer who can't raise a down payment out of savings is not all that certain to be able to make his payments when due. That could lead to foreclosure, and not all states have laws favorable to mortgage-owners. Increasingly, though, second-mortgage borrowers are financially solid people seeking only to use some of the equity built up in their homes without having to refinance existing first mortgages—the bulk of the home's value—at record or near-record mortgage rates.

Where to buy a second mortgage: Mortgage bankers, realtors, attorneys specializing in real estate, and title-insurance companies frequently know when second mortgages may be available at any given time. And they can help with the legal paperwork involved.

Once you have bought, though, selling out isn't always easy. You may have to take less than the face value of the mortgage to attract a buyer; that would give him a return on his money that's even greater than the original interest rate on the mortgage note. On the other hand, if you happen to be the buyer at a discount, you can realize a return of 20%-plus.

***But don't lose sight of the risk that goes
with it.*** To be conservative, stay away from a second
mortgage that—together with the first already in place—
would bring the total in loans against the property to more
than, say, 85% of its appraised market value. And make sure
that the first mortgage is no more than two-thirds of the
amount of the second; this way, if you have to pay off on
the first, it won't be an intolerable burden and will be easier
to sell.

REAL-ESTATE SYNDICATES

They are really a form of direct ownership of real property, though they offer some of the convenience of securi-
ties-type investment. In effect, they are partnerships in a
property-owning venture. The organizer, or general partner, finds the property and does all the work of putting
together the deal for a substantial chunk of the equity; in
addition, he may take an acquisition fee of 10%, more or
less, as his compensation for finding and purchasing the
property. The limited partners are the investors who contribute the bulk of the money to finance the venture.

Purchasers of shares in a syndicate can realize yields of
15%, and sometimes considerably more, especially if the
mortgage terms are favorable and rental conditions are good.
In addition, there are the shelter benefits—deductions from
income for depreciation, taxes, and interest.

Essentially, there are two types of syndicates:

Private deals involving sophisticated investors in the
50% tax bracket who take one or more shares that can be
worth as much as $50,000 apiece. Such syndicates may in-
volve fewer than thirty-five participants and would therefore not require registration with the Securities and Exchange Commission or state regulators.

Public partnerships for less affluent, less sophisticated investors who purchase shares costing, say, $3,000 or
$5,000 each. These are registered with the SEC. Brokerage
fees of 8% or so are not uncommon in public and private
deals—another load your investment must carry. But these

costs need not make the deal look sour if the prospects are otherwise bright.

How can you participate? Ask your stockbroker; brokerage firms these days usually act as agents for public syndications—or know of those who do so. If you decide to participate, read the prospectus that you must be given—and read it carefully.

If you don't understand all the technical points or have difficulty with the numbers, ask your attorney or certified public accountant to review the entire deal. And, above all, have him check out the developer/syndicator—his reputation and any other deals he may have put together.

REAL-ESTATE INVESTMENT TRUSTS

These securities—sometimes called REITs—do offer investors a very liquid way of getting into real estate. REITs function like corporations, and some of their shares are listed on the major stock exchanges, meaning that they can be readily sold at any time. And they offer substantially the same tax advantages as real estate itself, as long as the trust "qualifies" by distributing 90% of its income to the shareholders.

REITs had their heyday in the four years just preceding the recession of 1974–75. Between 1969 and 1973, their assets zoomed twenty-fold, to $21 billion. At one time, they were making more than 20% of the real-estate construction and development loans in the country.

Starting with stockholders' equity, they would borrow from banks, insurance companies, pension funds, etc., and put the proceeds into real estate. At first, the emphasis was on buying and owning properties. But, as good ones grew scarcer, more and more went into construction loans and mortgages. Having too much money too soon led to bad investments.

Then the roof fell in when money got tight and those to whom the REITs loaned money got into trouble. When the borrowers couldn't meet their payments, the REITs had to take over. But then they found themselves with properties running in the red. Some billion-dollar REITs, sponsored by the biggest banks in the country, went bankrupt. In others, stockholders saw the value of their shares fall by as much as 90%. For a while, the term REIT conjured up pictures of unfinished apartments in Florida.

But the strong housing markets of 1977–78 improved the REITs' fortunes. Rental income increased, and inflation boosted the value of assets. Many REITs were able to swap cancellation of loans they owed for property they owned, reducing their debt and their interest costs, but also their capital. Sophisticated investors began to notice that the value of some REITs' assets was far greater than the market value of their stocks. They bought certain of the more solid trusts, and share prices rose significantly.

REITs are in better shape these days. Most of the 225 still functioning concentrate on equity again, where the profits can be higher, and which makes them less vulnerable to the problems of builders to whom they loaned construction money. Some REITs offer the extra attraction of giving investors the benefits of past losses than can make future distributions tax-free.

But note that REITs are still vulnerable to the impact of tight money. They still have to operate, at least partly, on borrowed funds, and high interest rates can hurt. Not much more than a third of REITs are really making money. Unless bought significantly below the value of the assets—and those assets are of quality that promises continued profitable operation—REITs should not be considered a conservative investment.

> **Where to buy them:** Any stockbroker can buy shares for you and, no doubt, get you industry reports on the leading performers.

MORTGAGE-BACKED BONDS

These are a relatively new but extremely attractive—and secure—investment for persons with a minimum of $25,000 to invest. In many respects, they closely resemble corporate bonds but, while they generally have been given AAA ratings, they offer the higher yields equivalent to those of an A-rated bond.

These securities are issued by large banks and savings and loan associations, who collateralize them—generally over-collateralize them—with collections of mortgages up to 175% or 200% of the face amount of the bonds. This makes them virtually disaster-proof; and the issuer remains responsible for principal and interest even if some of the mortgages do go into default. (The bonds do not carry a government guarantee as Ginnie Mae pass-through certificates do.)

The bonds must have a minimum maturity of five years under Federal regulations, with as much as eight years fairly common; at least one issue has come out for twelve years. They pay interest semiannually and are traded much like regular corporate bonds by major brokerage houses.

Offerings of mortgage-backed bonds are sometimes bunched in fits and starts. The flow tends to dry up in periods of tight money when the issuer finds it hard to round up high-enough yielding mortgages to put into the collateral pool.

>***How to buy them:*** Any brokerage house can buy
>them for you. If it is part of the syndicate offering a
>new issue, there's no commission. Otherwise, the bro-
>ker can buy a mortgage-backed bond in the secondary
>market at the same commission as a corporate issue.

CHAPTER SIXTEEN

OTHER TAX SHELTERS

FAIL-SAFE RATING ON . . .

Safety: Those that follow tried and true paths are quite safe; others can be disallowed by the tax collector.

Income: Returns, especially some years after the initial investment, can be good.

Tax Status: Tax benefits can be very, very large.

Every year, Uncle Sam takes a hefty bite out of the incomes of most Americans—and the larger the incomes the bigger the bite. There is nothing you can do to heal past wounds, but there are steps you can take to "shelter" this year's income—and that of succeeding years as well—from the tax-collector's grasp. The shelter aspects of real estate and real-estate securities were touched on in the two preceding chapters. But many of the principles hold for other types as well.

> To be sure, some tax shelters are especially suited for the really wealthy—people with investment income taxed at 50% to 70%—and the higher the tax bracket, the more that can be saved. But inflation has pushed even middle-income people into ever higher tax brackets, so tax shelters can also be worthwhile for those in the middle-income range. Besides lowering your taxable income, and tax liability, they can also yield a good return on your money as well as capital gains—rewarding pluses in an era when it's so hard to keep inflation from eroding savings.

The array of shelters available to investors these days ranges from the tried-and-true to the new and very exotic, some of which may not prove very practical—or acceptable to the tax collector. Real estate, of course, has been around for a very long time—and oil-and-gas ventures, too. But now the purveyors of shelters—the brokerage houses and specialized financial-planning firms—are outdoing each other in devising new areas and programs to meet the growing demand; it's a demand that gets bigger as inflation bites harder.

> Among the new ventures being offered to investors are participations in drilling rigs to be leased to the oil companies for exploration, jet aircraft and helicopters, and research and development projects. At one point in 1980, Merrill Lynch, the brokerage firm, was even exploring the possibility of acquiring baseball's Chicago

White Sox for syndication to shelter-seeking investors; but this deal never went through.

All shelters have certain elements in common—features that let them take advantage of favorable provisions of the U.S. tax laws. These may be loopholes to critics, but they are godsends to the knowledgeable and the burdened. Such provisions include the investment and energy tax credits, rapid depreciation and generous depletion allowances, interest deductions that permit leveraging with borrowed money, and the lower capital-gains rates. In the early years of a shelter's life, before income begins to flow, an investor's share in the project's operating losses can be taken as a deduction from his other income.

The value of a tax shelter can change, of course, as the tax laws are amended. As bracket rates are lowered, the exemption may be worth less, though it could still be very appealing.

Note that there is usually some risk attached to the typical tax shelter—in some cases, a great deal of risk, which isn't often clear to the nonprofessional investor. No shelter is as safe as a Treasury security or, say, a Certificate of Deposit from an insured bank or savings and loan. The economics of a venture could go sour; bad times could cut the venture's income, but interest on borrowed money must still be paid, nevertheless. And the Internal Revenue Service could disallow the deductions that the shelter offers.

There are also future tax consequences to be considered. Most tax shelters are long-term investments. Some time down the road, you will be getting cash distributions. If you are going to be in a higher tax bracket in those future years, the extra tax you pay then will, at ordinary income rates, wipe out at least part of the savings you make on this year's shelter.

IRS is increasingly on the lookout for what officials term "abusive" tax shelters—those that are designed primarily to confer tax benefits, rather than to make a legitimate profit. If there are doubts about the intention to make a profit, there may be serious doubts in the tax collector's mind about the validity of the claimed deduction. Or put it still another way—if it isn't a good investment, the chances are fairly good that it won't fly as a tax shelter, either.

> So you shouldn't go into one with money you need to live or retire on or educate the kids; it's not wise to mortgage the old homestead to put the funds into a shelter. But we will try to indicate the degree of risk involved in the various types of shelters in the pages that follow.

Note, too, that shelters no longer offer quite as much in tax savings as they did in the happy days before Congress passed the Tax Reform Act of 1976. Except in the case of real estate, that legislation limited the deductions an investor could take to the amount of money he had "at risk"—that is, to his own cash or capital he borrowed and is obligated to repay. Until then, he could also deduct "nonrecourse" loans—often loans secured only by the assets of the venture, for which the investor was not personally liable—or money borrowed from the general partner to be repaid only out of the project's income, if any. Pre-1976, shelters often provided first-year write-offs that were several times the investor's actual commitment. One result of the 1976 Act, for example, has been to limit the use of coal and certain other shelters.

> Congress and especially the Internal Revenue Service are constantly trying to curb shelters further, though beneficiaries keep mounting more or less successful efforts to retain some of the old basic standbys. The "minimum" tax of 15% that can be levied on so-called "tax-preference" items has already gone far to assure that even the most successful shelter-investors pay *some* tax. (See the Glossary on Page 181 for definitions of

tax preference and other terms.) The IRS can also, under certain circumstances, "recapture" tax benefits previously taken. And it is constantly attacking schemes it considers dubious, so much so that the U.S. Tax Court has tried to consolidate dozens—even hundreds—of cases into single actions in order to lighten its load.

Before getting down to specifics, let's make a distinction between investments that give you tax-free income and those that offer offsets against the taxes you owe on income and capital gains from all other sources. The first kind was discussed in Chapter Ten. The second group includes real estate, oil and gas ventures, and other more exotic types that permit deducting up to twice as much or even more of your initial investment from other, current income.

> *To make the distinction clear,* let's say that you put $10,000 into a municipal bond paying 7%. Your *future* income of $700 is tax-exempt. And if you are in the 37% tax bracket (taxable income of $29,900 or more under the tax law in effect during 1980), the tax saving to you as against a taxable bond would be $259. But if you put the $10,000 into an oil and gas venture giving you a 70% write-off, you would be able to deduct $7,000 from *this year's* taxable income—for a tax saving of approximately $2,500 under the 1980 tax schedules. Of course, your municipal bond will be saving you that $259 year after year over the life of the bond if your tax bracket and the law don't change, while the oil deal may yield no further expense deductions after the second year (though a real-estate venture could). But, hopefully, you'd be getting royalties as wells come into production, and part of the royalties would be sheltered by the depletion allowance. What's more, you would be able to realize income by reinvesting the $2,500 you sheltered.

As noted in the chapter on real-estate securities, tax shelters generally take the form of limited partnerships or what are called syndications. They are usually set up to operate for a set period of years, often seven to twelve. One or more general partners put the deal together—finding the opportunity, handling all the legal and other arrangements as well as the books, and making all the decisions. The limited partners are the investors who put up the money but otherwise play a passive role. They get their respective shares of the net income, their portions of those all-important tax deductions and, in the case of real estate, their piece of the potentially significant appreciation in the value of the property—that is, capital gains. They are usually responsible only for the amount of capital they originally agreed to put in.

The two types of syndicates that are often used in real estate, private deals and public partnerships, are characteristic of other types of tax shelters as well.

Getting into a tax shelter is simple in concept. You merely write out a check and sign some forms. But choosing a rewarding and relatively safe type calls for considerable care. A reputable brokerage firm or your accountant or lawyer may be knowledgeable in this area or can tell you who the good syndicators are. Whomever you choose, it's important that your adviser be someone in whom you can have confidence and with whom you can be comfortable—that is, whose judgment you can respect.

Generally speaking, the best time to go into a shelter is early in the year, before the good ones have been snapped up. You would also get the maximum tax benefits in many cases, where the deductions are prorated for the period of the year you have been involved. Here is the story on the broad array of tax shelters available.

REAL ESTATE *is not only the most popular of tax shelters,* but probably the safest as well because there will be durable and tangible assets—land and buildings—behind your investment. Even at times when the real-estate market is weak, its very softness may create opportunities for general partners to acquire properties at bargain prices that can rebound with a subsequent business recovery—and with continuing inflation. At the risk of repeating some of the points made previously, it's worth looking into real estate again because there are a number of aspects that didn't surface earlier.

Most real estate shelters share certain basic advantages—all operating costs involved can be deducted from the rental income along with a write-off for depreciation. There are several possible depreciation formulas that an investor can elect. Under the simple straight-line method, the Tax Code permits owners to divide the purchase price by the property's useful life—say, eighteen years on "used" residential property—to get a 5½% annual deduction. But there are also accelerated-depreciation formulas which permit the taking of one-and-a-half times the straight-line amount (in the case of commercial properties) and as much as double (for residential).

> • *But there is a potential string tied to the accelerated-depreciation privilege—the "recapture"* by Internal Revenue of all or a portion of the tax savings resulting from the difference between the use of accelerated and regular depreciation; on the sale of the property, that difference would be taxed as ordinary income, rather than at the more favorable capital-gains rates.

Real-estate shelters can be classified into four subgroups, each with some variation of the benefits—and pitfalls—common to all. One would include commercial properties. The other three: older properties that are rehabilitated; conventional residential projects; and government-subsidized housing developments.

There are two types of real-estate shelters that many investors find especially appealing:

The rehabilitation of commercial build-

ings at least twenty years old offers investors still further tax breaks, in addition to the basic advantages—and disadvantages—that all commercial property enjoys: These extras include a 10% investment-tax credit in the year the improvements are made. Note that a credit is subtracted from *taxes,* while an allowable deduction merely comes off *income* before the tax is computed.

Government-subsidized housing is one of the most attractive investments for individuals. Usually, money is invested in installments over as many as five years, during which deductions for depreciation and interest run between 150% and 250% of the yearly investment. Eventually, as much as 300% of the total investment can be written off. But the lack of liquidity is even greater than is the case with other real-estate ventures. Because these developments generally involve low-rent apartments for the poor and elderly—the object of the subsidy—there is only a minimal annual cash flow of 1% to 2% and limited potential for capital gains in the later years of a project's life. And any excess depreciation resulting from an accelerated method must be treated as ordinary income if the interest in the property is sold in the first 100 months of purchase. After that, the amount recaptured decreases by 1% per month, until there is no recapture after 200 months.

> Raw land may or may not be an interesting speculation, but it isn't a full-blooded shelter because it can't be depreciated. It can, though, provide interest deductions on the money borrowed as well as capital gains.

OIL AND GAS DRILLING *ranks after real estate as a popular tax shelter.* It is riskier, but can provide a greater return, in part because the price of crude oil has increased tenfold over the past decade from about $3 a barrel in the early 1970s, while drilling costs have risen only 100% to 200%. In addition to all other advantages, a shelter that rides up with the cost of energy is a fine inflation hedge.

There are three types of oil and gas drilling

ventures. The riskiest are the **exploratory** programs—sinking wells in promising but unproven ground; only about 12% of all exploratory efforts are successful. **Developmental** efforts involve drilling in the proven areas where hydrocarbons are known to exist; such programs usually entail a minor fraction of the risk of exploratory programs. **Balanced** ventures combine both exploratory and developmental efforts, with the overall degree of risk falling somewhere in between. Risk can often be reduced by diversification of the investment over dispersed drilling locations.

Along with increased risk can come increased potential return. Some estimates indicate that, over a twelve-year period, oil and gas projects will provide a substantial annual return, depending on the risk taken—plus the valuable tax shelter.

Oil and gas operations offer three kinds of tax advantages.

• **Intangible drilling costs,** which include the labor, chemical, and drilling-site preparation and actual drilling expenses. They are deductible and could account for as much as 70% of the cost of completing a well.

• **Depletion allowances** that are a percentage of revenues from the sale of the oil and gas, not to exceed 50% of the net income from the investment. (The percentage allowed was originally 22%, but is dropping.) These offer much of the benefits of depreciation in real estate.

• **Capital gains** which can be realized after two years, when the majority of the deductions have been taken. The investor's interest can then be sold, or traded for stock, with the proceeds taxed at the more favorable capital-gains rates, subject to possible recapture of intangible-cost write-offs.

Let's say you buy a $10,000 share in a developmental oil project that proposes to drill about a dozen wells in a proven field. In the first year, you could deduct 80% of your investment, including intangible drilling costs; accordingly, you would be reducing your taxable income by $8,000. In the second year, you might well get an income-distribution of 5% of your investment from the first crude to flow in the venture. The oil-depletion allowance would enable you to deduct the permitted percentage of that—say, for example, 22% or $110. And you might be able to deduct most of the last $2,000 of your investment. These deductions could shelter the $390 not covered by the depletion allowance, as well as up to $1,610 of other taxable income. In the subsequent years in which the wells continue to produce, your income would go on, and you could deduct for depletion every year.

But some offsetting disadvantages should not be ignored. The risks of losing your investment in dry holes is great enough to have led most of the states to take protective measures requiring that investors have substantial net worths—say, about $225,000—and/or taxable incomes of perhaps $60,000 before a venture could accept their money. In addition, some of the intangible drilling costs taken could be treated as a tax preference on sale of the interest. Investors cannot write off more intangible drilling costs than their original investments. (No similar limitation on deductions presently exists for real estate.)

The Windfall Profits Tax Act, which Congress passed in 1980, has spawned a new crop of energy-related tax shelters, by-products of the effort to encourage the development of substitutes for imported oil. Promoters are now offering units in ventures that propose to build and/or operate wind-driven turbines, low-rise hydroelectric dams on swift-moving streams, plants for processing wood, stills for producing alcohol for gasohol, systems that recycle waste-gas pollutants, and the conversion of sawdust and wood chips to several kinds of fuel. Investment units often run about $50,000 or more each.

Much of the allure of these new shelters is the additional tax credits—as high as 15% of the investment—that can be taken, in addition to the 10% long available on virtually all types of productive equipment; in some cases, then, the credits alone promise to return a big chunk of the investment in the first year. And there are also Federal subsidies to make the projects economically viable. But, as you'd expect, the bigger payoffs are linked with bigger risks: The technology involved in most cases is still untested. If the venture fails, you would not only lose your investment but would have to cough up some of the credits taken, besides.

EQUIPMENT LEASING *is the third major way to invest in tax shelters.* It involves the buying and leasing to users of equipment such as boxcars, fishing boats, computers, larger medical devices and so on. The fact that a minimum investment of $25,000 is often required, though, may limit this type of shelter's appeal.

The main tax advantages offered include the right to take the one-shot 10% investment tax-credit — though that can be a subject of negotiation between the group of investors and the user — as well as the depreciation at accelerated rates for both new and used equipment. It is not unusual for first-year deductions to exceed 150% of the original investment. Additionally, these ventures could provide a steady flow of income.

As you'd expect, there could be potential problems: The equipment could become obsolete, killing the chance of a capital gain. In a recession, demand for the items such as boxcars — and the income they generate — could slump or even vanish; that occurred in many cases in 1981. What's more, depreciation and tax credits could be recaptured if the equipment is sold within a limited period. Also, the investment credit and possibly the interest deductions could be lost if the equipment is leased on a net-lease basis, where all or most of the expenses other than the interest and taxes are paid by the user. Finally, the investor is personally liable for the money borrowed in his name to finance the equipment purchase and also for storage and maintenance costs should the equipment he owns stand idle.

For the purposes of illustration, let's look at boxcars. A number of brokerage firms have been selling such shelters lately to individuals, rather than partnerships. As noted, they have by no means always been a great success, but here's how they might work for you: Suppose you buy a car for $40,000, with a 20% down payment of $8,000 and a loan for the remainder at, say, about 14% a year. The boxcars can be written off according to a variable schedule under the new Reagan depreciation proposals. Your 1981 depreciation deduction would come to about 11%—or $4,400. Then there would be the deduction for the interest on your loan—$4,480—for a total of such write-offs in the first year of $8,880 or tax savings of $3,286 for someone in a 37% tax bracket. Adding in the 10% investment credit reduces your tax liability for 1981 alone by another $4,000 and the total tax savings becomes $7,286. That's 58% of the $8,000 plus $4,480 in interest that you put up the first year. In future years, there'll be no investment credit, but you'll continue to get depreciation and the same interest-rate deductions.

Equipment-leasing programs involving data-processing systems or medical equipment work in much the same way as the boxcar venture. With heavy leverage—large amounts of borrowed money—deductions of as much as 300% of the original equity investment are possible. But the big loan feature adds big risks to these ventures: One is the fact that such big write-offs could catch the tax collector's eye. Then, too, because of the rapidity with which improvements are being made in such high-technology items, the equipment leased could quickly become obsolete, thereby eliminating any income. And you'd still be liable for repaying your share of the loan—plus interest.

THERE ARE STILL OTHER KINDS OF SHELTERS that are not so widely known or used. They are largely vehicles for wealthy investors willing to take high risks.

Major motion pictures have been syndicated as tax shelters to groups of about twenty-five investors. Each puts up, say, $170,000 over three years, and obligates himself for loans of an additional $500,000 to $600,000, the money being used to pay the producers and to advertise and market the film. Using a special depreciation method allowed for motion pictures, investors can depreciate the major portion of a film's costs over the first two years. Since the marketing costs—perhaps 40% of the total—are concentrated in the months immediately after the picture is released, they can be deducted fairly quickly. In addition to the deductions, investors may take the investment credit and distributions of income in future years, after the production and sales costs have been recouped. TV, cable, and perhaps videodisk sales could in time beef up the return further.

> The deal sounds good even if the film should prove to be a turkey and fail to earn its production and distribution costs. The fact is, though, that the investor runs the risk that Internal Revenue will seek to disallow the deduction if the Service concludes that the deal is designed to generate tax benefits rather than to further a genuine business purpose. The fact that promoters have a positive "opinion" from a law firm is no guarantee that the deal will pass IRS scrutiny.

Breeders and feeders are two programs involving livestock, usually cattle. **Breeding** programs are the less risky. They offer a 10% investment-tax credit on the animals bought. First-year deductions that can amount to 200% of capital are also possible for depreciation and feed costs. Offspring can be sold for taxable income, while proceeds of the sale of the breeding stock are taxed as capital gains. But the risks are large: cattle-price fluctuations, disease, and high operating costs.

Or an investor can buy cattle to **feed.** All the costs are paid up front—and are deductible. A first-year deduction can total 200% of the investment. There is also a possibility of solid profits when the cattle are sold—or losses, if the cost of feed goes up or cattle prices go down. And profits are taxed at regular rates, not as capital gains. In both programs, deductions are limited to the capital actually at risk—excluding loans for which the investor is not personally liable.

Charitable donations provide shelter opportunities through purchase of art or jewelry at wholesale prices. The pieces are then donated to a museum or library, with the current market value of the item taken as a deduction. But Internal Revenue is increasingly suspicious of such deals and recently refused to allow deduction of the inflated costs of Bibles bought at wholesale, held for a year, and then donated to religious institutions.

Still other, less frequently used tax shelters, involve timber and cable TV. Others will doubtless be cropping up as economic conditions change.

One last note: It can't be stressed too often or too strongly that you should get the opinion of a qualified lawyer or accountant before you consider *any* tax shelter; the prospectus that details the venture will probably be complex and hard for a nonexpert to really understand. Your consultant, though, can at least point out the risks. You ought to inspect the property yourself (in the case of real estate) or bone up on the area (in the case of oil and gas) or learn something about the technology (in the case of equipment). And remember: The more glowing the prospects of savings, the more cautious you should be. Generally, real-estate ventures will prove most suitable—and safe—with development-type oil and gas ventures next, and equipment leasing perhaps after that.

Here's a final check-list of steps that you—or your attorney or accountant—should take to avoid undue risk.

- **Make sure that the general partners you go in with are honest,** capable, and have good track records.
- **Make sure that the project is economical-**
- **ly viable—**that you can show that you will make some money in addition to getting write-offs.

- *Make sure that the shelter is structured soundly*—that it conforms to the tax laws for maximum benefits.
- *Weigh the attractiveness of the tax savings* to one in your bracket against the dangers of things going wrong.

GLOSSARY OF TAX-SHELTER TERMS AND PROVISIONS

Minimum Tax: The Tax Code now levies a tax on the income from certain "preference" items to try to make sure that all taxpayers pay at least some tax. These items include intangible drilling expenses incurred in getting oil and gas wells into production, some part of the oil-depletion allowance, and accelerated depreciation of leased property. The tax is 15% of the total of such amounts that exceed the greater of $10,000 or one-half of the "regular" tax for which the taxpayer would be liable.

The At-Risk Provision: You cannot take loss deductions for amounts that exceed the money you have invested — your equity plus borrowed funds you are obliged to repay. This is really the money you have "at risk." Real estate is specifically exempt from this rule.

Recapture Provision: Internal Revenue may recompute and "recapture" some of the extra tax savings from depreciation at greater than straight-line rates, if you sell your share in a shelter in the first 200 months of its life, or possibly for a longer period in the case of commercial property. There is a similar provision for intangible drilling costs on productive oil and gas wells.

Percentage Depletion Allowance: A percentage of the value of the oil and gas sold—up to 50% of the net income before depletion—can be deducted from income. The concept is similar to that of depreciation—the using up of an asset, in this case the oil and gas in the ground. The allowance is falling, stepwise, from 22% to 15% by 1985.

The Limit on Investment Interest: The amount of interest payments that you can deduct each year on money borrowed to finance your shelter investment is limited to the sum of your net investment income plus $10,000. So, if you have interest payments of $13,000 on a loan for an investment and have net investment income of $1,000, you can only deduct $11,000 in interest expenses ($10,000 plus the $1,000 income).

Long-term Capital Gains: The profit on the sale of your share of an investment is subject to tax at capital-gains rates. If held for less than a year, the rates are actually the same as ordinary income rates; if you hold the asset for longer than a year, though, a more favorable set of rates comes into play: 60% of the gain goes free of tax, and the rest is taxed at your normal tax rate, with a maximum overall rate of 28%. So if you have a gain of $10,000 and are in the highest bracket (70%), you would be exempt for 60% of the gain—or $6,000—leaving $4,000 to be taxed at 70% . . . or $2,800. Proposals to reduce the capital-gains tax rates have long been pending in Congress.

SECTION IV

SPECULATING INSTEAD OF INVESTING

CHAPTER SEVENTEEN

GOLD, SILVER, AND DIAMONDS

FAIL-SAFE RATING ON . . .

Safety: Unlike almost all other places to put money, gold's degree of safety lies in the eye—and emotions—of the beholder. Silver has a somewhat more solid base in industrial demand.

Income: Gold itself yields no income, though gold stocks do. But many believe that buying and holding gold and silver will pay off even more than it already has, though there is no guarantee of this.

Tax status: Profits from buying and selling are subject to capital gains taxes.

As the ranking above clearly suggests, gold (and silver, too) is a thing apart from bonds and stocks and mutual funds. Its centuries-old mystique and deep psychological allure make it unique; it may not even warrant the term "investment." Whether it does or not depends on how you choose to look at it, and what you expect it to do for you. In the end, this is the only meaningful test as to whether or not gold has a place in your scheme of things. This is why this chapter is necessarily so different from all those that precede it.

For the most of this chapter, we'll be talking in terms of gold. But, in almost every statement made, the word "silver" could easily be substituted. Gold-minded investors—or speculators—often are interested in both, and for the same reasons. The fact that the industrial demand for silver is in far more delicate balance with the supply than is the case with gold gives a more substantial rationale for its price increases, but still does not by itself account for the steep rises of recent years.

Diamonds have a lot in common with gold and silver as glamorous but volatile investments. The big price increases of recent years have been of similar orders of magnitudes. But diamonds differ from gold and silver in the size of the market, the minimum investment "units" and the way they are marketed. That's why they will be treated separately at the end of this chapter.

Gold probably should be among your assets if you take a dire, gloomy view of the future. If you think that the world is going to pieces in a hurry, then you may feel more comfortable owning gold in some form or another, as a safe store of value for at least some of your wealth, especially against the possibility of total collapse in the value of paper money. If you feel that our political leaders' ineptitude will ultimately make all paper assets worthless (or nearly so) or that our and/or other governments may topple into revolution, then knowing that you possess a universally accepted store of value may be very reassuring, indeed. Gold is a compact, easily carried asset, less susceptible to government confiscation than other forms of wealth, and easily converted into other assets without embarrassing questions. Whether its price zooms one month and falls the next may not be your most important consideration. Possessing gold may provide a measure of insurance against ultimate disaster.

At any rate, many people seem to think so; gold has been a sensitive barometer of public anxiety for many years now. But there are those who wonder whether, in an anarchic world, you'll be allowed to keep your gold, once you take it out of the vault and try to spend it: Won't the lawless take it by brute force? And will paper evidence of gold ownership be worth any more than a Treasury bond, let alone be negotiable?

Some other considerations come into play, if insurance against collapse of the world as we know it is not your main objective. How effective can it be as a hedge against inflation? How safe will one's principal be? What sort of return can one expect, in capital gains or income—if any? And which of the several ways available is the best way to buy gold?

There is no doubt that anyone who bought gold at the start of 1979 had no cause to regret it. Its price rose from $217 an ounce in January to top $800 in early 1980. It fell back from that level to below $500. That still represented sharp gains over the price prevailing before 1979. And what happened to those who bought near the top and did so on borrowed money? What many investors have to ask themselves now is: Where will gold's price go from the level obtaining at the time they are considering a purchase?

But its volatility is not the main reason for skepticism about gold. The major reason many give for avoiding anything but a token commitment to gold (or silver) is the lack of any meaningful justification for price rises of the magnitude that occurred in the Seventies.

To a considerable extent, its price at any time goes to where buyers and sellers collectively think it should be.

That, in turn, depends on their perception of supply and demand trends, political uncertainty, as well as the rate of inflation in key countries of the world.

Industrial demand for gold and its use in jewelry is rising, to be sure, while production of new supplies is leveling out or declining. But, if viewed strictly as a metallic commodity, there need be little cause for alarm because, unlike silver, present supplies are ample to meet this sort of demand for many decades. And cheaper substitutes are being devised for certain uses.

Now, let's examine those other factors at work in bulling the price of gold: Uncertainty . . . those fears of catastrophe enumerated above . . . erratic shifts in selling by Russia and South Africa . . . the heavy buying by the increasingly wealthy Arab oil producers . . . and the accumulation by the Doomsayers' disciples. To the extent that this last cause is a factor, the advice to buy gold is a self-fulfilling prophecy: Buying is itself a force that tends to move the price higher and so many feel justified in staking more on the advice—which tends to move it higher still.

But, as its price behavior in the latter part of 1980 showed, these factors don't always work toward pushing gold higher. A strengthening dollar, stepped-up Russian gold sales, and a suspension of Arab acquisitions showed that price declines are also possible. And what would happen if such declines should shake the faith of some of the Doomsayers' followers—especially those who financed part of their purchases with borrowed money? To the extent that they decide to bail out, a price decline could be accelerated.

So it is too simplistic to say that, since rapid inflation is likely to plague us for years to come, the price of gold must necessarily go up. Its rise in recent years has far exceeded the rate of inflation in the U.S. and, on average, in the world as well. Gold isn't just a barometer of inflation.

As for political impact, the war in the Middle East was still going on toward the end of 1980, the Russians were still in Afghanistan, and Ronald Reagan's election spelled the end of the Salt II Treaty. Yet gold broke below $600 at the time of his election. In other words, gold was moving down, despite ongoing uncertainty around the world

To be sure, for considerable periods, there was some explanation of its behavior to be found in oil. Gold does seem to rise with oil prices, which kept rising steadily. One basis for the linkage lay in the fact that Arab oil producers were wary of all currencies, not just the dollar, and so they diverted much of their incoming revenues into gold—though, more recently, they have done some selling, too.

In addition, many around the world use gold as an inflation hedge. And there are those, noted above, who prize it for its insurance aspects. As gold's following—and its price—have risen, it has gained a greater degree of respectability. Some leading banks have now become involved in the market in several ways. And foreign central banks are believed to be buying gold, if only to shore up the value of their own vast holdings.

It would be foolhardy to predict that gold will get very much lower any time soon—let alone get back to $35 an ounce. Those who bought large quantities on its way up—and foreign central banks that keep so much of their reserves in gold—are hardly likely to risk depressing its price by disgorging, no matter how much they might like or need to at some future date.

It would be equally rash to say that gold's price can't keep going higher—that it can't reach $1,000 or even $2,000 an ounce before we are all very much older. It could and might; but, also, it might not. Betting on the oil cartel to raise their prices further—and betting that the West won't get its inflation or energy problems under control—does not seem like a foolish wager at all. This is why even some who don't fear the worst from oil or disaster are tempted to extend the principle of diversification to gold. This is why some who are not dyed-in-the-wool gold bugs suggest keeping 15% to 20% of one's assets in gold (or in silver).

The point is that no one really knows—not even the Doomsayers in Chapter One. Some less doctrinaire gold bugs have long since concluded that gold's price has already exceeded all reasonable limits and that its future is too risky. After all, the gold market is much like any other market, subject to powerful, often unanticipated forces that can sweep the price in either direction before you see what is happening and can react.

To put your fortune into gold is to bet on the behavior of producers like the Russians and hoarders like the Arabs. You may think that you can foresee their behavior. But do you really feel that sure they will continue to behave as they have in the past when the world is changing so rapidly? (Incidentally, all that's been said about gold applies to diamonds and similar assets—in spades.) What would happen if a substantial number of holders decide that the world isn't going to fall apart in three years and got tired of waiting for their gold to go higher? Suppose they decided to sell. Its price would crash and no one could predict the bottom.

But suppose the Doomsayers are right, and the country will experience a great Depression in two or three years—what will happen to the price of gold then? The Depression of the early Thirties saw prices collapse—a severe deflation. Maybe it won't happen this time; our relatively moderate recessions failed to bring prices to heel, perhaps because the world has changed. But a wave of deflation could occur again, for all anyone knows, if people can't buy the goods the country can produce. If it did, wouldn't gold come way down, too?

This is why many thinking people still hesitate to jump on the gold bandwagon. They cannot bring themselves to view gold as a productive investment or to commit significant amounts of wealth to an asset that is subject to frequent and irrational price movements prompted by sudden shifts in speculative thinking.

Here, more specifically, are some of their reasons why:
• **Gold is not an earning asset.** It pays no dividends or interest.
• **Gold is costly to keep**—to store and insure, and in the sense that the income from investing in a bond or stock is foregone. Many jurisdictions impose sales taxes on the purchase of gold coins.

- *Alternative means of buying gold (see below) involve risks*—for example, if a sudden decline in the price forces a margin call for someone using borrowed money. Remember what happened to silver. In thin markets, such as those of gold and silver, it wouldn't take a tidal wave of selling to depress the price severely.

- *And there is always the danger that the Arabs will shift their buying* from gold to some other asset—a heavier interest in the stocks of American companies, for example. They wouldn't have to dump their present holdings—just cut their buying significantly—for a major prop to be knocked from under the present price.

- *Gold's price has already discounted inflation for many years to come,* if special factors like the Arabs' buying should cease to operate. And if the world should find itself in a severe depression—perhaps because the oil producers squeeze the world economy too hard—deflationary forces would also be set in train: What would they do to gold's value?

- *How much of a profit would you make if gold did rise to $1,000* from, say, $600? About 67%. The increase of tenfold and more is behind us. It can be argued that the potential for gains that exceed 67% in the next three or four years is greater in carefully chosen common stocks than it is in gold.

You may conclude that gold is still a fairly good investment for you, after weighing the factors that could push its price higher against those that could hold the price down. The question of insurance against disaster is an element that should not be dismissed lightly by those for whom it is a nagging concern. For those not so concerned, a token commitment might be the most that seems prudent, especially if made on a substantial dip in the price. But, as noted, that's also something of an emotional decision.

Here are the common ways of getting into gold—we are deliberately avoiding the word "investing"—with the advantages and pitfalls of each:

Coins are one of the simplest ways to get into gold—for example, British Sovereigns, French Napoleons, Canadian Maple Leafs, or South African Krugerrands, the latter containing exactly one Troy ounce of gold. They can be bought at many banks at the day's market price of gold, plus a commission of 5% to 8% and often a sales tax. They are easily stored in a safe-deposit box and are readily salable. And they are more flexible than a gold bar; they can be sold in small units—a part of your holdings at a time.

Bars are usually for larger purchases, and take less per ounce in commissions—say, 3%. They come as small as a kilo—32½ ounces—but 100 and 400 ounces are the standard sizes. Bullion should be stored and insured and may have to be assayed (or analyzed) on resale, at a charge. It cannot be sold piecemeal like coins. Bullion is subject to sales taxes in many states, and can be purchased for you by quite a few banks and brokers. And it, too, earns no income.

Stocks of U.S., Canadian, or South African gold-mining companies are one vehicle for getting into gold that does yield income in the form of dividends—sometimes at rates as high as 20%. Prices of the shares move up and down with the price of gold, as well as—in the case of South Africa—with the political situation. There are no insurance, storage, or sales taxes involved in owning gold-mining shares, other than the usual brokerage commissions you would pay on any stock. Prudence suggests diversifying any gold-stock investment over several companies—and countries—to spread the risk of physical disaster or political upsets.

Certificates issued by leading banks, such as Citibank of New York, are receipts for quantities of gold bullion purchased and held for the account of the buyer, who does not have to worry about its physical possession. The minimum purchase is $1,000 though buyers can thereafter add to holdings with as little as $100 at a time. Citibank charges a commission that varies up to 3%, depending on the size of the purchase. There is also a 1% fee for selling or making delivery, plus a storage-administrative charge of ½% after the first year. These certificates yield no income.

Futures offer the greatest opportunities for profit in gold—and the greatest risks of big losses. The market in contracts works much like all the other futures markets.

(See Chapter Eighteen.) The margin required is around 5%, and there are no storage or delivery costs because transactions are usually closed out before contracts expire. Futures provide no current income, either; the profits come from selling out at a higher price. The commodities departments of most large brokerage houses can buy or sell gold futures for you.

As noted, some of the zeal for gold has spilled over into the markets for silver and platinum. Silver, for example, has at times shown even sharper percentage increases in price than gold. But, while silver is also a precious metal, its price is subject to forces that operate differently than they do on gold. For one thing, relatively more of silver is industrial metal; unlike gold, it is not ardently acquired for hoarding. For another thing, because demand presses so heavily on supply, its price can be influenced by manipulators.

The stories of the fabulous profits in diamonds of recent years must cause even conservative investors to wonder whether they're missing a good thing. And, in fact, a serious look will show that there's more than merely glitter to fine gems. But, by their very nature, they are not for everyone. And even if they do fit one's investment strategy, the buyer had better beware how he goes about getting in.

The amount invested in diamonds each year in the U.S. is now more than $300 million; it has quadrupled in just a few years. Though prices pause now and then, many experts in the field view slowings as only temporary and offering good buying opportunities.

If the future is like the past, carefully chosen diamonds may be very rewarding long-term investments. During the Seventies they outperformed vehicles like stocks and bonds, and have far outpaced inflation. Over the past ten years, diamond prices have risen 15% annually—25% in 1979 alone. High-quality gems—the only kind worth investment—have done even better. Appreciation has been relatively steady, without gold and silver's gyrations. One fine stone which cost $1,200 in 1969 was worth $18,000 in 1978 and $60,000 early in 1980 and was still valued at about $55,000 later in the year after a softening in prices.

And the diamond-sellers say that there are still good reasons for being "bullish" on diamonds.

• *Buying interest is growing* as knowledge of diamonds' performance spreads, along with their value as an inflation hedge. Individuals are now using diamonds in Keogh, Individual Retirement Account, and other retirement plans.

• *The supply is kept limited.* DeBeers Consolidated Mines, the cartel that dominates the world market, controls supply tightly to ensure rising prices.

• *What's more, diamonds are more salable* than most other "collectibles" such as coins or antiques, though less so than stocks, bonds, or gold. And they can easily be stored in a ready-at-hand safe-deposit box.

But wonderful as it sounds, investing in diamonds is really only for a limited few. Here are some of the reasons why:

• *First, the cost.* You would have to pay close to $9,000 or $10,000 for the lowest-quality diamond that experts would deem suitable for investment; the most rewarding gems would require a much larger commitment.

• *Second, you ought to have a hefty net worth* before you even consider purchase of an investment-grade diamond. Because they are not as salable as stocks and bonds, diamonds should not be more than, say, 15% of your assets excluding your home; you should have $50,000 in assets before you consider gems. If you want to buy a top-quality stone—at say, $55,000—your portfolio should exceed $250,000.

• *Third, you have to hold stones for at least two to three years* to get a really super return. So you have to be prepared to sit tight even when value is going up by only a little. And you can't let yourself panic if there is a temporary setback such as has occurred at times.

• *Fourth, a diamond will yield no income* while you are holding it.

• *Fifth, a slowing in the underlying infla-tion rate will lower the value of your invest-ment,* since diamonds are seen largely as an inflation hedge. The lower the value, the harder it is to sell a gem.

• *Sixth, past performance is no guarantee of future increases.* The market could just dry up for any number of reasons that now seem remote.

If you decide diamonds can fit into your program, and if you think that the potential for gems outweighs the risk, you still have to proceed with the greatest care. Many inves-tors have paid dearly for mistakes in buying or for failing to deal only with reputable sellers. Here's the way the ex-perts — people who have spent their lives in the diamond market — urge you to proceed.

Choose only diamonds of investment quali-ty—diamonds that measure up according to the four C's: Carat, Color, Clarity, and Cut. (See the Glossary below for the meaning of these terms.) Buy the very best stones that you can afford — generally a one-carat size or larger; don't go below G or H in quality, though the actual price of any stone will depend on its own unique characteristics.

Get your diamond certified twice—once by the seller but (and this is vastly more important) also by the Gemological Institute of America. GIA certification will cost at least $80 and take three to six weeks, but it's worth it because it helps ensure resalability. If the seller won't agree to GIA certification, don't buy.

Shop around for the best price. It can make a big difference. Check Sunday's *New York Times* or Monday's *Wall Street Journal* for rough — but only rough — guides to going prices. Consider using a broker to find the best deal — he'll be worth the 5% to 10% fee; your bank or accountant may be able to help you find one near you. Make sure it's clear that the brokerage fee is — or is not — included in the price and that the seller will resell the stone for you later, if you ask.

Make sure you deal with a reputable firm, one known to your bank or lawyer. Be sure it is registered in

your state and has been in business at least three years. And
never buy from an ad or a phone pitch without checking
the seller's reputation. One final word: If the deal sounds
too good to be true, it probably is.

*   *   *

GLOSSARY: The four C's used in establishing the value
of diamonds.

Carat: The unit of weight for gems—1/142 of an ounce.
There is a growing market for stones of about a half carat,
but it's best to invest in at least a carat.

Color (or lack of it): The best and most colorless gems
are designated "D," but "E" and "F" also rate high. "G" and
"H" have slight color, and are considered the lowest in investment quality. Color can account for half of the value of
a stone of given weight.

Cut: The shape of a piece, with round considered the
best. Cut accounts for about 25% of the stone's value.

Clarity: The degree of flaw. "FL" means flawless, the
best. VVS1 and VVS2 are slightly clouded, though still
worthwhile. Clarity accounts for 25% of value.

CHAPTER EIGHTEEN

COMMODITIES

FAIL-SAFE RATING ON...

Safety: The risk of loss is enormous. A commodity speculator can lose all of the capital he commits.

Income: There is no fixed rate of return, though profits could be very large.

Tax status: Profits on commodities futures qualify as long-term capital gains, even if held only six months and a day, in contrast with twelve months on, say, stocks.

By its very nature, commodities trading—that is, commodities speculation—lies outside the focus of anyone who is concerned with safety of principal and steady income. But there has been so much written about the gyrations of the commodities markets and so many new ways to play the game that an investor can be pardoned if his curiosity is piqued. This brief discussion of commodities trading should not be considered an endorsement, though. Quite the contrary.

There's no denying the fact that more and more investors are being lured into commodities by the prospect of turning a small investment into a big profit while enjoying a lot of excitement along the way. But it takes a special kind of investor to play the game. The typical speculator must be ready to lose on most transactions in the hope that he'll make those losses back—and a lot more—on the occasional combination of timing and judgment that brings a 25% or 50% or even 100% return.

A speculator can reap his profits in a variety of commodities: metals like copper, tin, lead, and zinc; farm products like corn, wheat, soybeans, orange juice, and porkbellies; lumber; and now financial instruments such as Treasury bills and Ginnie Mae certificates. There are numerous U.S. commodities exchanges, the Chicago Board of Trade being the largest.

Trading commodities is really trading so-called futures. The speculator can buy a futures contract binding him to take delivery—and pay for—a given quantity of the commodity at a given price on a specific future date; or conversely, he can agree to sell a contract to deliver the goods. The exchange sets the amount of the commodity that underlies each contract—5,000 bushels for soybeans, for example, on the Chicago Board of Trade. And it also sets the minimum margin of cash that is required—$1,500 in the case just cited, in mid-1980—that is, 30 cents a bushel, which for much of the recent past has been less than 10%.

Only the commodity-using companies actually take delivery of the products; they are in the market to hedge

COMMODITIES   **199**

against violent swings in the prices of things they buy, process, and sell in the ordinary course of their business. But speculators generally sell out—or buy back in—before the contract is due to expire, taking their profits or suffering their losses.

> Financial institutions, including banks, will use, say, Treasury bill or Ginnie Mae futures to hedge against interest-rate fluctuations that can depress the value of their fixed-income securities holdings. If there is a decline in market prices, the profits from the contracts they sold offset the losses in market value. Commissions paid are a modest "insurance premium."

As noted, if you call the turn correctly, the profits can be large. A 10-cents-a-bushel rise in soybean prices could mean a profit of more than 15% on the money put up in the case of the speculator with, for example, 5,000 bushels of soybeans.

> Let's say that he bought the contract with a $7.00-a-bushel price, putting up $2,500. A 10-cent-a-bushel increase gives him a profit of $500 on his 5,000 bushels—on paper so far, at any rate. After deducting $65 for commissions, in and out, his net profit is $435. And $435 on a $2,500 investment is 17%.

On the other hand, a 10-cent-a-bushel drop would wipe out 23% of the commitment—the $500 loss, plus $65 in commissions on his $2,500 investment. And a 50-cent drop would clean that speculator out entirely, though chances are his broker would sell him out well before that point is reached, unless he decides to put up some cash—that is, more margin.

But a 50-cent decline is not out of the question. It could easily happen in a fairly short period in the giddy markets that exist today, even though there are limits to the price moves permitted in a single day. This is why commodities are no place for the conservative investor. No one can be sure when the report of an unexpectedly large crop in our Midwest or the Russian Ukraine will come along to clobber wheat prices. Or a potential upheaval in Africa could send copper prices zooming—right after you sold a futures contract. Chances are that the big-time speculators will have heard about it—and acted on their information—before you did. Their buying and selling can drive the prices up or down.

The various commodities exchanges have devised new ways in which individuals can participate in the futures "action" with limited exposure and professional guidance.

One way is the publicly offered commodities fund or "pool," a vehicle which many securities firms have been establishing and promoting. They resemble mutual funds in that the money of many persons is used to buy a number of different kinds of futures—as many as twenty-five different commodities and delivery months. The firms' commodities departments usually execute the orders of an independent trading manager who makes the selections and determines the crucially important timing of purchases and sales. Some houses sponsor specialized funds—say, for currencies or gold only or for grains and other farm products.

> The minimum amount an individual must put up varies from $1,000 to $5,000, depending on the fund. In addition to the brokerage commissions the sponsoring firms get management fees, and incentive payments—that is, shares of any profits. Customers can often withdraw their funds on a week's or a month's notice, though some funds will only redeem at the end of a quarter.

Each fund must supply a prospectus to potential participants, listing among other information its past performance. The prospectus should be read carefully.

A variation on this idea is the individually managed account, for those willing to commit substantial amounts; such accounts could, of course, lack the diversification of the pools, but profits could be larger—and losses, too—in very speculative special situations.

> Somewhere in between are the private pools that involve commitments of $10,000 up to $100,000 or more, which are offered to limited numbers of a firm's customers.

Commodity options are still another device that the brokerage industry has been trying to get off the ground, in the face of skepticism of the regulatory authorities who question the commercial function such options may have. A law passed in 1978 has had the effect of limiting the number of firms that could offer such options and permitting them only in gold, silver, or copper.

> Commodity options resemble stock options in that they represent the right to buy a futures contract for a relatively modest premium. A pronounced move in the price of the underlying commodity could bring a big profit, while losses are limited to the amount of the premium. Officials have been reluctant to broaden their interpretation of the law to permit wider commodity-option trading because of the potential for abuses.

Here are some rules you ought to consider, if you still think that you would like to take a flyer and that you would like to try it on your own:

Make sure that you go in with money that you can well afford to lose—nothing like your nest egg for retirement or the down payment on a new house.

Be prepared to spend a lot of hours and effort learning the ins and outs of commodities trading. It need not be a full-time occupation, but it could come close. You can't just buy corn or wheat or copper and forget about it for a few months—or even years—the way you can a Treasury bond.

Bone up on two or three specific commodi-

ties that you'd like to deal with, since—for all their simi-
larities—each product is unique. Make sure that you line
up a steady source of current, up-to-the-minute factual information on the fields you have chosen—*The Wall Street
Journal* and/or *The New York Times*, government crop reports, perhaps a newsletter or trade magazine in the field,
and so on. A number of brokers put out informative commodity letters. And there are books you can buy, seminars
you can attend.

Shop long and carefully for a broker who
strikes you as a person you can work with, in whom you
can have confidence, and who will take the time to help
you learn. The firm that buys and sells your stocks or
bonds—or any large brokerage firm—will probably have a
commodities department. Check the recommendations that
several make in their letters or verbally against what actually happens to develop rough but comparable track records
of their judgments and knowledge.

**Play the game on paper for as long as it's nec-
essary** for you to feel that you have an understanding and
grasp of what's going on. See that you can show an overall
paper profit over, say a three- to six-month period.

Don't rush in before you are ready. But once
you are in, be prepared to be decisive—to cut losses, once
you discover that you misjudged the particular situation.
Don't try to hang in just to vindicate your judgment.

As you get more deeply involved in commodities trading,
you will come across exotic types that have only been
meaningless names heretofore—Treasury bill and bond,
currency, and those Ginnie Mae futures, for example, or
porkbellies. And new types are being proposed all the time.
Despite some reluctance to grant approval by the Commodities Futures Trading Commission, the various exchanges
have pushed contracts for a number of different kinds of
futures including three-month certificates of deposit, the
Standard & Poor's 500-stock index, two-year Treasury notes,
six- to ten-year Treasury notes, and three-month Eurodollars. (Eurodollars are dollars held outside the U.S. and subject to international market factors.)

Essentially, financial types work the same way as any future, but you may find that some are closer to your long-time interests and, therefore, are more comfortable or congenial to work with.

Each Treasury-bill future contract bought, for example, entitles the buyer to take delivery on $1 million worth of three-month bills at some future date. Margin required is about $1,500. For every move of a "basis point"—a hundredth of a percentage point in the discount rate on the bill for which the contract is written—the investor makes or loses $25. But Treasury bill rates—in the actual market as well as futures trading—have been known to move more than 50 basis points a day. That could mean a profit or loss of $1,250—83% of the initial investment before commissions—in a single day.

> Remember the point made in the chapter on fixed-income securities: It is close to impossible to pinpoint the turns in interest rates, but precise timing is everything in commodities-futures trading. If a rising or falling interest-rate trend is so clear that you feel confident about what's coming for the next few weeks or months, the market has probably discounted the likelihood—fully.

As you delve even more deeply, you will learn about sophisticated variations of the commodities-trading game. Spreads or straddles, for example, can serve to limit your losses—and also your profits: They involve buying for delivery at one future date, while selling an offsetting contract in the same product with another date. The prices of each may well move in the same direction, but possibly at different rates under different influences. And it's the difference that can create the profits opportunity—if you are right in playing the longer-term factors affecting prices against the shorter.

> Pyramiding is another practice that some commodity speculators use to beef up profits further. They take

gains from successful trades and plow them back into additional contracts, increasing their base for further profits—but for losses, too.

Summed up, commodities trading can be exciting and, if you are lucky as well as smart, it can be profitable. But it can be ruinous, too. One of the smartest professionals in financial futures quadrupled his $2 million capital in less than a year—but then lost it all in a few days back in 1979. In other words, commodities trading is hardly Fail-Safe Investing.

CHAPTER NINETEEN

COLLECTIBLES

FAIL-SAFE RATING ON...

Safety: The risk involved in investing in collectibles is, except for the most knowledgeable experts, as great as any you can take.

Income: By their nature, collectibles do not throw off income. The return is the profit on the ultimate resale.

Tax status: Capital gains treatment for objects owned for more than a year.

Inflation always generates distortions in economic decision-making and strange behavior on the part of people who try to protect themselves against its ravages. One avenue that many are pursuing these days with far more vigor than ever is collecting—antiques, art, jewelry, silver, Persian rugs, stamps, coins, rare books, Christmas plates, and even comic books, baseball cards, and beer cans. Some dealers estimate that three times as many collectors are sinking twice as much money into exotic collectibles as they were, say, two years ago.

Appetites have been whetted by tales of the large increases in prices that such objects have commanded—15% a year or even 20% a year; that's as good as or better than money-market funds are paying. Indeed, prices of Persian carpets, no doubt given an extra boost by the threat to new supplies from the unrest in Iran, have zoomed even faster. Collectibles have appealed to many as a wonderful way to beat inflation—and then some.

But it ain't necessarily so. There are great dangers in investing in collectibles—unless you know exactly what you are doing. Officials of some of the biggest firms that deal in such objects warn that the average uninitiated investor is a loser. He tends to hear about the shining prospects after the smart money has already enjoyed the price run-ups, and he gets in after the profits have been made. With so many unsophisticated investors rushing in, prices become distorted and unstable.

There are pitfalls on every hand. To invest successfully in fine paintings or sculpture, for example, you really have to be an art expert—or know one on whom you can rely. There are really no short cuts—certainly not those "you can't lose" buy-back deals advertised so heavily in class magazines.

> The typical pitch asks you to buy, say, a painting at a given price with the guaranteed right to sell it back to the dealer within a specified period at your original purchase price. And it does sound good. If the picture's value goes up, you can be well ahead of the game; if it

doesn't, you get your money back. You can't lose—
right?

Actually, you can. Such a deal is probably no bargain. To begin with, as in the case of diamonds, only the
finest pieces in any of the arts appreciate significantly—and
you are not likely to be offered any of these under the typical buy-back plan. Then, too, even if you sell back at the
original price, inflation will have eroded the value of the
money you get back; and you would have lost the dividends
or interest it could have earned.

This isn't to say don't buy art. But do so because you like
it and want to live with it. Let any investment appreciation
be a bonus.

***The pitfalls of investing in all types of col-
lectibles are deep.*** It's easy to get stuck with a cheap
imitation or a specimen of poor quality and little value, if
you don't know what you are doing.

***Fads change, and items that cost a bundle
can come plummeting downward*** when you
least expect. You may have to wait several years to show a
profit. You start behind because even a reputable dealer can
charge you 50% or more above the wholesale price; that's
not an unusual markup for merchandise.

Getting your money out is often a problem,
when you need cash or want to take some profits, unless
you are dealing with traditional, widely bought and sold
objects. You may find that it takes months to find a buyer—
if you can find one at all, except at a give-away price. You
can shop around for the dealer who will pay the highest
price. But don't be surprised if he only gives you 50% or
60% of what you paid; he has to make a profit on the resale.

***This doesn't mean that you must shun col-
lectibles*** like the plague. Some, like rare stamps, coins, or
paintings can now be legally purchased for Keogh-type individual pension funds. If you feel that you still want to go
ahead, here are some rules to follow seriously:

Buy only objects that you like for their beauty
and the pleasure they give you—articles that you can vi-

sualize holding for an extended period of time. That way you can ride out fall-outs in the market.

Bone up on your subject. Read the books of the leading authorities in the field and also the trade magazines—*Linn's Stamp News, Coin World, Antiques Magazine,* etc.

Shop around; haunt the auction sales; talk to dealers. Keep at it until you feel that you know what constitutes quality and a fair price and how to spot flaws.

Don't go out shopping until you feel reasonably confident of this—that you can tell the difference between cut crystal and pressed glass. Age of an object and name of the maker do not automatically guarantee quality. But rarity, combined with a broad demand, does offer good prospects of profit.

Then, buy only the best—the very top quality. This means choosing a truly fine 9 x 12 foot Kerman among Persian carpets rather than a bigger, but less elegant piece at half the price. This applies to silver, antiques, stamps and coins, etc. Really fine pieces are far less likely to lose value and are far more likely to appreciate.

Use an expert as an adviser or broker when making a substantial purchase, if you aren't absolutely sure of what you are doing. He'll know value and will be worth his relatively moderate fee.

Insist on certification of authenticity when buying furniture, Indian jewelry, and the like.

Deal only with established firms, even though you will have to pay a good-sized markup. Be skeptical of auctioneers who set up shop in motel rooms and are gone by the time you discover a problem.

Learn the pitfalls in caring for the particular kind of items you collect. Polishing rare coins, for example, can fuzzy the images on their surfaces and sharply reduce their value.

How to find an expert consultant: Ask your banker for the name of a reputable consultant in the field. He can probably refer you to an established dealer who can buy, sell, consult, or broker for you. Leading auction houses will sometimes give you reliable appraisals.

CHAPTER TWENTY

SCAMS AND CONS

People with money to invest are increasingly bombarded with promises of returns that will far exceed going rates. The galloping inflation, which leaves little if any true income left after the erosion in the dollar's value is taken into account, makes such deals all the more attractive—and investors all the more receptive. But the combination of alluring rewards and pressure to stay ahead of the game can be dangerous to your financial health.

There is no such thing as a free lunch.
You don't get something for nothing.

Except in most unusual circumstances—if you are lucky to find them—high, once-in-a-lifetime rewards go hand in hand with high risks. And high risks mean that you can lose as much as—if not more—than you can make. So let your skepticism rise with the richness of the promised profit. Many who would never buy snake oil or the Brooklyn Bridge have been known to go for equally foolish "scams" involving land, oil and gas, gold, diamonds, and even such offbeat flyers as wine and frog-legs growing. Those who let greed overwhelm their good judgment usually live to regret it.

The financial history of this century is littered with cases in which clever con artists were able to fleece countless investors by promising rewards that could not be justified on any rational basis. The late Charles Ponzi gave his name to an entire species of schemes that offered returns that were, literally, "too good to be true."

A Ponzi scheme is simply one in which the money put in by new investors is used to pay dividends to some who invested previously; that way, the promoter is projecting the illusion of a highly successful and profitable operation. Actually, though, he is robbing Peter to pay Paul in a recurring, increasingly frenzied cycle that ultimately has to break down. In a classic case, the promoter will promise his victim 10% or 20% or even 50% on money invested for only 45 or 90 days or some such short period. The funds may never even go into the project in question; there may not even be a project—except on paper. However, the promoter will pay off the initial investors, punctually and fully—but with cash taken in from newer investors. When word of those first payoffs gets around, still other investors come swarming in, while many of the original "marks" beg to reinvest—and even to put in additional funds. But let the stream of new victims slacken, or someone ask to see the project or its books, and the whole house of cards will collapse. Only those who got out early—and then stayed out—will be able to boast of a profit. Most of the others will lose all or at least a great part of their contributions.

Ponzi's particular con, in Boston back in 1920, was, ostensibly, to buy "postal-reply coupons" in Spain for a penny apiece and redeem them at U.S. Post Offices for a dime. Those who put money into the scheme were promised a 50% profit in forty-five days. All told, 40,000 investors ponied up $15 million over an eight-month span. No one questioned the simple logic—or illogic—of the scheme until a local newspaper discovered that less than $1 million in postal coupons were issued during the time that Ponzi was supposed to be committing that $15 million. When new suckers backed off and investors demanded their money back, the scheme collapsed. Ponzi spent ten years in jail and died in 1949, broke.

In some modern-day Ponzi schemes, even the initial investors often get nothing back; they don't expect any payments during the developmental period, and after that it is too late. But many contemporary scams are Ponzi schemes, in essence. The principle, if that's the word, is at the heart of a broad variety of swindles that have just recently been used to bilk the unwary. Unfortunately, it seems to work in every field — or, to put it another way, every legitimate investment seems to invite a phony clone.

Here is a sampling of just some of the scams that could be aimed your way at any time. Some of them are so cleverly carried out that they might have led the master himself to salute his contemporary imitators. In most instances, the cases that follow are only examples of the kind of swindle that could be occurring in a particular field of investment; all too often, there are numerous, ingenious, and costly variations on the theme.

Land: Crooked operators have found that land is a fertile field for fleecing investors. In one case of the purest Ponzi, a prepossessing thirty-year-old Long Island man was indicted for swindling more than 2,000 persons from as far away as California out of at least $15 million. He and some associates promised that investors would get their money back — as little as $1,000 as well as sums approaching $200,000 — within ninety days, with 20% interest. Their money was going into "short-term real estate" and "performance bonds" — two nonexistent types of investment. The promoter had dazzled his victims with a life-style garnished with a Rolls-Royce and private jet (both rented, it turned out). When the bubble burst, he fled the country — with most of his victims' money.

The more conventional type of land "scam" has involved companies the names of which were built up into household words — which sold hundreds of millions of dollars in virtually worthless parcels to unsuspecting customers. Deception and high pressure were used to peddle hundreds of thousands of undeveloped acres in the Southwest to investors all over the U.S. and abroad. The company all but guaranteed the land to be superior as an investment to stocks and bonds or savings certificates. Prospects were dazzled with the promise that the property's value would rise 20% a year, and there were vague company mutterings about buying the land back if the customer so desired. Needless to say the utilities, shopping centers, and recreational facilities were never fully built as promised nor did urban areas grow out to provide the promised resale market. Government agencies eventually moved in to halt the misrepresentations and even seek restitution, but thousands of buyers ended up sadder, wiser, poorer—and stuck with worthless land.

There are more than 6,000 individual land-development projects in virtually every state registered with HUD—the U.S. Department of Housing and Urban Development—and these are only the ones with fifty or more parcels to be sold across state lines. No doubt most of those are legitimate, giving buyers all that's promised. But note that HUD has suspended some 2,500 developers' activities since 1972.

The point to remember is that the potential variations on the theme are literally infinite. In some swindles, the investor's money really does go into an office building or warehouse—at a price inflated by the promoter, who may also divert the rents to his own use while letting the mortgage be foreclosed. Or take the case of the Florida operators who sold tax shelters that were supposed to be investments in cultivating and distributing horticultural products. But only a minor fraction of the investors' cash actually went into horticulture; the rest was looted wholesale.

Oil and Gas: There is probably as much variety in oil cons as in land. The granddaddy of them all—up to now, at any rate—seems to have been the great Home-Stake Oil swindle in which hundreds of investors were taken for an estimated $100 million or more in a phony oil-drilling scheme that was carried on by its promoters for the better part of a decade. Its victims included the very top names in many fields—high-bracket superstars in entertainment, politics, business, and even law and banking. It was a Ponzi operation, pure and simple. Only a small part of the funds was actually used to drill for oil; the great bulk was siphoned off by the promoters in many ways.

It was one of the slickest examples of the genre. Prospects were inundated with thick, chart-and-statistics-filled reports on drilling sites, financial projections, and technical studies of the recovery methods to be used. It was far too much for successful, busy people to read—and they didn't. Instead, they relied, they thought, on the judgment of other prominent people who had already signed up—a fact that the promoters trotted out in selling a potential investor. After a year's steady stream of optimistic progress reports, replete with geologists' analyses as well as an occasional dividend check, many signed up for another year. In a large number of cases, the tax shelter was the most important consideration—the write-off of intangible drilling costs and later on the percentage-depletion allowance. But, when the Internal Revenue Service found that wells really hadn't been drilled, some of those tax benefits had to be disgorged.

Several similar scams were carried out on almost as large a scale by two companies named Geo Resources and Petrofunds, which proved to have a strong attraction for leading sports figures. In other instances, "boiler rooms" jammed with telephones have been used to solicit investments across the country—again in phony or nonexistent properties.

In one day alone in the winter of 1980, Federal and state officials filed civil fraud complaints against thirty companies engaged in selling "spot crude-oil delivery contracts." To begin with, these were illegal, unregistered futures contracts, in the view of government officials. But, in addition, the promoters were accused of "making false and deceptive reports and statements concerning the expected profits . . . and the risks involved." And the operators certainly didn't tell the investors that most of the money went into commissions, rather than into buying the oil that was supposed to be delivered to customers to make the profits.

Coal: The same sort of schemes that are worked for oil and gas are used in phony coal-mining ventures. At one time in 1980, the U.S. Attorney in just the southern district of West Virginia had seventy fraud investigations going, and twenty convictions under his belt. One of the victims was a local police chief who specialized in lecturing on how to spot frauds.

Gold: The sharp rise in gold prices of the past few years has encouraged dozens of con artists to devise numerous schemes to separate eager investors from their money. Some operators have dusted off one of the oldest swindles known in this country — bringing the victims caught up in the gold fever to worked-out mines in the far reaches of, say, Arizona, to see for themselves the rich veins of gold. In fact, the mines were "salted"; the flakes of gold were sprayed on by a shotgun blast. By the time the investors learned the score, the promoters were long gone.

Other operators, often graduates of land and other swindles, use "boiler-room" telephones to sell so-called forward or deferred delivery contracts. One outfit would make more than 10,000 calls a week to names on a purchased list and would hint at having millions in bullion stashed in well-known banks. The investor's money — $10,000 or $20,000 or even many times that much sent in by mail to a salesman he never met — was to be a down payment for one or more 100-ounce lots of gold which he could acquire at a future date when the price goes up — as the promoter's nonexistent research department assures it will. The investor then exercises his right to buy the gold at the earlier price. In theory, he can then sell it, or the contract itself, if he doesn't take delivery, and pocket the profit. As things turn out, though, the investor — and thousands like him — discovers that his payment was largely a nonrefundable fee entitling him to nothing. And he could also have been told that some of the rest of his money was lost in a sudden, adverse move in gold's price.

Government officials have termed those supposedly risk-free investment vehicles "commodity options," which have long been illegal, except in the limited circumstances mentioned in Chapter Eighteen. Agents try to shut down these boiler rooms and freeze the assets of the promoters. But, all too often, by the time the complaints are filed, the crooks have skipped.

The same sort of swindles are perpetuated in silver and coins, too. Only the details are different—as in the cases in which brokers and dealers took investors' money to buy silver coins but either never did so or didn't buy all that they promised. Sometimes the promoters booked more orders than they could fill and tried to cover by trading—speculating—in futures. Sometimes they just took the money and ran.

Diamonds: In the past year or two, diamond scams have been competing vigorously with land frauds for the dubious honor of claiming the most victims and stealing the most money. They also rely heavily on the telephone and high-pressure misrepresentation. Investors are called cold by companies with impressive names like DeBeers Diamond Investment Ltd., a close copy of the South African diamond cartel, with which the swindle has no connection whatever. The victims are told that fine gems have been appreciating at 30% or 40% a year and are promised quality diamonds (or rubies or sapphires) at cut-rate prices with money-back guarantees. The number of otherwise careful or cautious persons who responded, sight unseen, with $5,000 checks in the mail would astound you.

In actual fact, the stones delivered will be highly flawed and low quality or even zirconium or paste—if you get delivery on anything at all. You would not be able to verify quality if you did get the gems because breaking the seal nullifies the guarantee. The appraiser's certificate you get is a worthless phony. As for the money-back guarantee, try to find the promoters to collect it. This is why officials in a dozen jurisdictions are investigating dozens of companies, many headquartered in Arizona, which have already fleeced thousands of investors of more than $100 million.

The reality is that investment-quality diamonds—and any asset worthy of the word—are never sold by telephone. What's more, only the finest gems, usually of one carat or more and of the finest color and cut, appreciate in value; a price of $30,000 to $50,000 would not be all that uncommon. Anything else you buy is no more than costume jewelry—and no doubt 50% to 100% overpriced at that. The best appraiser's certification to go by is that of the Gemological Institute of America.

One could write a thick and weighty book about the endless variety of swindles that abound to trap the gullible—and, yes, greedy—investor. But let's just briefly sketch some of the others of which investors should beware:

• **_The wine scheme_**—This was a one-of-a-kind operation only in the sense that the particular product ostensibly involved may never figure in another such scam. But substitute any other word and you could run into a similar scheme at any time, because this one was pure Ponzi. A young telephone-company official sold investors promissory notes to pay 20% to 100% in profit over an eight-month period, with the money to be used to corner the market in low-quality "industrial" wine from Portugal to be resold to American food-processors as an ingredient in salad dressings. The scheme lasted for a decade, lured in bankers, lawyers, doctors, and hundreds of little people, and cost investors as much as $100 million. New funds were used to pay off early investors, though many actually reinvested. But there is no such thing as industrial wine.

• **_Securities frauds_**—Well-dressed,   fast-talking salesmen offering tremendous deals in tax-exempt or other securities have brought, instead, tremendous losses to numerous investors, including many who should have known better. In one instance, a banker was given a sheaf of municipal bonds, supposedly worth $1 million, as collateral for a

short-term loan of a third of a million dollars to a little old
wealthy lady with a tax problem. The investor was to get
the tax-free income over the life of the loan, plus a good-
sized fee. In the end, though, he was stuck with the bonds,
which turned out to be worth less than half the amount
loaned.

• **Pyramid schemes**—These are not the ones that
ask you to send a dollar—or even $50—to the names on the
top of a list. Rather, they are glorified franchising schemes
where the unit of investment may be $5,000. The "prod-
uct" could be a line of cosmetics or a self-help course, but
the scam really centers about selling wholesale-territory
franchises—at high-pressure pep rallies—to buyers who in
turn sell smaller areas to other investors who, in turn, sell
even further subdivisions, etc. The walls come tumbling
down when the numerous franchise-holders at the end of
the line find that there are no more franchisees around and
that the product itself is unsalable.

• **Truck-fleet partnerships**—The promoters sold
participations in tractor-trailer operations as tax shelters but
often didn't even buy the trucks. Rather, the money was
siphoned off—through service companies supposedly providing insurance, housing, computer, and legal services.

• **Pseudo-religious scams**—The "Church of Ha-
beem" founded by a "minister" with a $10 mail-order, Doc-
tor of Ministry degree lured hundreds of the greedy to "do-
nate" $500 apiece or more to become "Ministers of In-
crease." They expected to be rewarded, in three months or
so, with three or four times as much in return, even though
the promotional brochures specifically stated that the program "offers no expectancy from an investment, security or
stock offer." Silly as it sounds, many people took out second
mortgages and cleaned out savings accounts to participate.

It would be comforting to be able to believe that these
frauds belong to a bygone era—that they can't happen to
you in this day and age. But that's not true. Scams are being

run right now—today—though we won't know them for
what they are for some time yet, after it is too late. There is
simply no guarantee that the era of the fast-buck artist is
over. He will be around as long as greed and gullibility
exist.

**Swindles similar to those detailed above
could happen again,** despite all the laws that are
passed and the best efforts that regulatory agencies are making to protect the public. New schemes seem to be invented
faster than protection against them can be devised. The Securities and Exchange Commission, for example, can't always prevent fraud, especially when it hasn't had a chance
to find out that a scheme has begun to operate; it can only
swing into action when complaints from the public alert it
to a situation—though by then, as noted, it's often too late.
Besides, some swindlers regularly file reports with the Commission, ostensibly complying with its "full-disclosure" requirements.

**Scam victims can't always blame them-
selves too harshly, though.** The essence of a successful financial swindle is a compelling plausibility—at
the moment of decision, at any rate. And the professional
con man is an expert in his calling who is hard to resist.

As a rule, he is extremely personable—nice-
looking, warm, the kind of person you would really like to
get to know. He is earnest, sincere, and apparently has your
best interests at heart. And he projects an aura of success, so
he is the kind of guy you would *like* to get involved with.
Above all, there are no suspicious "vibes" that put you on
your guard. (If there were, he wouldn't be such an artist and
wouldn't have been so successful in extracting money from
his victims.)

**Fraudulent promoters usually have a con-
vincing, satisfying answer** to almost any question
that the prospect may have. Actually, though, much of
their success stems from the fact that the "mark" or "pi-
geon" is so hungry to be enjoying the promised goodies that,
in his eagerness to sign up, he doesn't even think of asking
the questions that he might in buying, say, a new TV set

costing a fraction of the money he's going to invest.

It is often hard for a nonprofessional investor to find the catches, the flaws, the outright lies that ordinarily alert him when he is heading into trouble. This is not to say that some "hot deals" won't be legitimate and pay off handsomely with no loss of principal. But they are likely to be few and far between; they are not likely to last long, once word of the situation's rewards gets around and others' willingness to pay more to get into the game brings the return down into a more normal and realistic range.

There is simply no substitute for knowing what you are doing—for taking the time necessary to assemble the facts and background you need to enable you to distinguish between the real and the fake.

When you are offered a deal that is out of the ordinary, be suspicious, no matter how sincere and persuasive the salesman may be. If he's legitimate, he won't be the least upset if you say you are going to ask for advice from others; indeed, he'll urge you to do so.

You can do a little preliminary screening yourself— before you get the word from your lawyer, accountant or banker—by observing a few simple rules.

• *Don't let the salesman rush you.* If he sets a deadline by which you must act, back off. Tell him to get lost.

• *Check the track record of the promoter.* (Your lawyer or banker or Better Business Bureau may be able to help.) Has he been successful in his past ventures? Ask for references—the salesman's and the company's— and talk to the people listed; ask them how his past deals have worked out. Smart investors do this all the time.

• *Make sure that the general partner has a real stake*—money of his own to lose—in the venture he is setting up, unless he is someone you have worked with before. You don't want him to be able to make money from commissions and management fees while you are risking your cash.

• *Don't deal with anyone strictly on the ba-*

sis of a telephone call. Ask to meet him — at his office rather than your home. Find out how he got your name. Ask for his banker's name and call to check up.

• *Ask for a complete proposal in writing—* the specifics of the deal; how much you must put up now and later; what you are likely to get back; and the commissions, fees, other charges, or guarantees involved. (Your lawyer will want these, anyway.)

• *Above all, do as much homework as you can* on the particular kind of investment before you do anything at all.

SECTION V

GETTING GOOD ADVICE

CHAPTER TWENTY-ONE

WHOM CAN YOU TRUST?

Even if you have a clear idea of your investment goals—where you want to go—you still have to work out how to get there. You may feel that you have the ability to plot the route yourself as well as the time required to do so. If you can, that's the best way to go; no one else can know your situation—your needs and resources—as well as you.

You may not even need anything more than common-sense advice on a particular point or two—the kind that your lawyer or accountant can give you in a matter of minutes. But perhaps 10% of Americans would be better off with a full financial plan. The fact that you felt a desire to read this book suggests that you may be among this number.

But many investors, perhaps yourself included, don't have the time to spend on financial planning—on keeping up with the new opportunities and devices that are coming along almost every day; those in their pre-retirement years are too busy earning an income to manage what they have already put aside. Or they don't have the patience for—or the knack of—making wise investment choices on their own. They don't trust their own judgment in these uncertain, fast-moving times. They need help and should face the fact that they do.

The problem is where to find a reliable source of the kind of help you need. The solution can be as important for your long-term financial health as the selection of particular investments or the timing of your purchases. An incompetent or inexperienced adviser could cost you major chunks of your capital.

But whom to trust? You can't just be guided by the impression that a prospective investment counselor makes or even by the plausibility of the investment philosophy he expounds. The woods are full of "experts"—some successful, some not. Some are charlatans, some sincere. And the advice you may get from one could be the diametrical opposite of the wisdom from another. Some—like many of the Doomsayers—insist that gold and diamonds are the only things in which to put your money; get out and stay out of the stock market (or real estate). Others say it's real estate (or stocks) but don't touch gold. They can't all be right at any one time.

Ideally, you ought to have your own personal financial counselor who gets to know your case—the particular circumstances unique to you alone—and stands ready on call to guide you with the best advice whenever you need it. He or she would be like the doctor or lawyer on whom you have been depending for many years. But finding one who is right for you probably won't be easy. And he could be expensive, especially if he's good.

A word of warning, though: Anyone who wants to be an investment advisor can be one and call himself one. The fact that he is registered with the U.S. Securities and Exchange Commission or with regulatory agencies in various states doesn't mean that he is competent or even honest. All you have to do to register is fill out a form and pay a relatively modest fee. No examination to take for the SEC or many of the states. No experience required. Just don't be a convicted felon.

It should be noted that you probably are already getting the benefit of professional money management indirectly, in ways you may not even realize. The insurance company that wrote you an ordinary life policy is investing part of the premium for you. (See Chapter Five). And the cash you put into a mutual fund is getting similar handling. But what about the rest of your capital? You may still want—and need—help in investing that. And that's where an adviser can come in.

Not all investment advisers are alike. In effect, there are two distinct categories, though both go by the same label and promise the same results.

One group, numbering only in the hundreds, might be called the purists. They provide advice and information only. They'll begin with a more or less exhaustive analysis of the client's income, assets, aims, and investment philosophy. Then they'll draft a financial plan with specific recommendations for making capital gains and/or boosting income, assuring adequate insurance coverage, financing retirement or children's education, and even making a budget. The advisers often are partnerships of specialists who jointly can select the particular stocks, bonds, tax shelters and other investments best suited to achieve the client's goals. And they may offer continued supervision, recommending sales and purchases to keep the program abreast of changing times.

These services don't come cheap. They take up a lot of the adviser's time. Some charge by time, and $100 an hour or more isn't out of line. Others set fees as a percentage of the assets under management or gear it to income or net worth. The total annual cost could run to several thousand dollars. Though the fees are tax deductible, and the advice may prove to be worth the price, the after-tax cost can be very steep for someone with only, say, $25,000 involved. This is why it's usually the wealthy who retain the purists—people with assets well into six figures . . . and more.

The other, far more numerous group consists of brokers, insurance agents, and bank trust officers whose primary concern is to sell a product. They provide advice "on the side," sometimes for a relatively modest fee and sometimes free, getting all or most of their compensation in the form of commissions on the securities, insurance, or trust and cus-

todial services sold. The advice they give could be good, but
you could also have cause to wonder about their detach-
ment and the potential conflict of interest between what
they have to sell and what may be best for you.

Assuming that you don't see your way to paying the first
kind of adviser's fees—or that you don't have enough money to interest him—how should you go about choosing from
among the second category? With little or nothing in fees
involved, there is no reason why you can't call on more
than one to get the benefit of the different sorts of expertise
they can offer. In effect, you can assemble your own staff of
specialists—a broker or bank trust officer for stocks and
bonds, a tax-shelter specialist, a real-estate expert.

The rules for choosing and working with these services
or advisers are essentially the same. Let's start by talking
about a securities broker and then note any special considerations for working with the rest.

***Choosing a broker should involve more
than calling the biggest firm in town and
asking for the first account executive who
happens to be free.*** Nor should you automatically
choose the house that charges the lowest commissions. Before you decide to take on a broker—or shift from the one
you happen to be dealing with—you ought to decide just
what you want him to do for you.

If you are of that rare breed who like to do it all themselves, you may only want an order-taker who will simply
carry out your instructions. Your search will be easy, if all
you want is a buying or selling agent and no advice. A so-
called discount broker is all that you'll need.

Discount brokers have mushroomed since the mid-Seventies, when the Securities and Exchange Commission de-
creed the end of fixed commission rates. The discounters
offer no services other than the execution of your orders.
And their charges reflect this; they can be half those of
"full-service" brokers—even less. If you don't want the services that the old-line houses provide, why pay for them?
Note though, that discounters often set minimum commis-

sions so that, for a small transaction, the fee could end up close to that of an old-line house.

Let's say that you want to buy 200 shares of XYZ Corp., selling at $19 a share. An old-line firm might charge $90 or more to buy the stock for you, and even more as time goes by and inflation boosts costs. But you could discuss the pros and cons of the investment with an account executive to your heart's content. A discount broker might charge half that or even less—but you couldn't talk about the market with him or ask him to check out the stock.

A glance at the ads back in the stock-quotation pages of *The Wall Street Journal* will on any day give you the names of several large and reliable discount brokers.

But if you do want advice as to what to buy or sell at a particular time, or guidance in the design of an investment program, you could well conclude that you want a full-service brokerage house—one that offers a bundle of services. You'll pay more in commissions, but if you are lucky you may get what you pay for. There's a lot more to think about if you go with a full-service broker who will help in decisions that can make—or cost—you money. To begin with, you'll want someone with whom you can feel compatible—someone who will take the time necessary to explain why he is recommending an issue and answer any questions that you may have. You'll have to use some judgment of your own, too, in deciding whether he makes sense.

But compatibility isn't enough. There is also the question of competence. It is as difficult to come to grips with as it is important. Years of observation of the species— as financial reporter as well as investor—have fostered a vast skepticism about the knowledge and judgment of the typical registered representative. Too many are "rip and readers" whose knowledge goes only as deep as what they grab from the morning wire report from the firm's head-quarters; these customers' men may look good and get by in a strongly and steadily rising market. But their limitations show up all too clearly when the turns come or in the up-and-down kind of markets of recent years that are also likely to be typical of the years ahead.

Some "reps" or the houses they work for have their pet theories and formulas—even computerized selection processes—that have worked for some periods. But by no means for all. If the picks were right 80% or even 70% of the time, these brokers would be too rich to bother with handling your account.

Actually, their records are usually spotty. Last year's most successful and celebrated pickers may bomb the next time out. But the customer who is seeking help doesn't always hear about the mistakes—which are always a result of the market's failing to perform as it was supposed to.

Even the pundits whose wisdom is eagerly sought out by the newspapers and TV news shows every time the market shows an unexpected bobble are really only life-sized and all too human when you get to see and know them up close. They may pore over their charts or tables or they may weigh what are called the "fundamentals"—that is, the basic economic trends that will affect an industry or a company. But they really can't see the future with any great clarity all or even much of the time. They simply can't always predict the twists and turns in collective human behavior that make markets go up or down—and make their trackers so frustrated. And all too often what vision they do have can be distorted by a need to justify—to themselves as much as to their clients and the world—their past predictions that have missed the mark.

The best performances in choosing stocks are usually turned in by analysts of special, sometimes fairly narrow, sectors of the investment spectrum; they do better than the generalists who try to predict the market as a whole. The more conscientious of these specialists steep themselves in the problems, of, say, the auto, computer or the petroleum industries, boning up on all aspects and going out to learn as much as they can, first hand.

An oil expert, for example, will no doubt visit drilling sites, talk to geologists as well as company executives, and become proficient in understanding technical reports. In many cases, they know as much about a particular industry as its leaders—sometimes more, because the analysts' perspectives may be broader. Their judgments are usually available to the customers of the brokerage houses they serve; indeed, some firms become known for their expertise in particular fields. Stories in newspapers like *The Wall Street Journal* or *The New York Times* can give interested investors a feeling as to which firms may be strong in given areas. If your broker is not a discount house, ask him for special industry reports the firm's research staff may have prepared. You are paying for them.

This isn't to say that every registered representative is just a glorified order-taker who really doesn't know what he is talking about. Some customers' men do take the time to learn, first, the client's needs, goals, and inclinations and then what the smarter specialists are doing and saying. They try to keep abreast of significant developments. Some even develop broad specialties of their own—for example, trading in options, tax-shelters, or fixed-income securities. The talented ones develop a "feel" for the market, especially the older veterans who can offer the invaluable experience of having lived through—and learned from—past market cycles. On the other hand, of course, the younger market men have grown up with the latest computer-related strategies.

Old or young, the really good brokers know their limitations. When you find one who promises little, but—after a trial period—does fairly well, you ought to stay with him.

Until you know this, though, you are flying blind. But you don't have to rely on intuition alone in choosing professional help. Ask friends or relatives for names of brokers who have served them well. Then check the names out with your bank, your accountant, or your lawyer; don't assume that because the man or woman is with a big firm that he or she is the answer to your prayers.

Speaking of big firms, they can often offer you more service for the same commission because they can spread, say, their research costs over a larger number of accounts. But they can be more impersonal, too—perhaps not especially sensitive to your needs. Smaller, so-called regional brokerage houses may be able to get with you more closely and can also alert you to opportunities in local companies that could prove to be rewarding investments. And some of these firms have records that are every bit as good as those of the nationwide giants. As a rule, though, in any firm, the larger your account, the more attention you are likely to get; indeed, some firms are not eager to take on small investors—say, less than $10,000 or even $15,000.

Here are some considerations to keep in mind in finding and dealing with a broker:

- ***Don't make your arrangement with a new broker strictly by telephone.*** Visit his office. Ask him about his investment philosophy, and for some specific recommendations and some of his firm's research reports. Ask for the names of several current clients and check them out; talk to them about what the broker has done for them. If he has earned a Certified Financial Analyst's certificate, you'll know that he is more than just an order-taker.

- ***Tell him what your investment objectives are***—income vs. capital gains, trading profits vs. long-term growth, etc. As noted in Chapter Two, a little reflection will clarify your own thinking and enable you to make your objectives clear to the broker. Write them up in the form of a letter to him, keeping a copy for your files.

- ***Be precise about the degree of discretion to buy and sell for your account*** that you wish to give—and put that in writing, too. The safest course is to give no discretion at all, requiring the broker to get your okay before buying or selling. You will come closer to achieving your particular objectives if you are involved in the decision-making. And your review of his recommendations will tend to limit "churning"—buying and selling to generate commissions; it will guard against rash—and risky—investment decisions.

- *Keep records of every transaction,* filing confirmations and monthly statements. Look at every communication from the broker as soon as you receive it, to be sure the execution conforms to your order.
- *Make sure that any of your funds that are temporarily idle will earn interest*—either from the broker or from an established money-market mutual fund into which the cash is automatically deposited.
- *And ask for any discounts from his regular commission schedules;* point out that you are a regular customer. Some big, full-service brokerage houses negotiate lower commissions under competitive pressure from the discounters. One, for example, will cut commissions as much as 40% while another cuts as little as 10%. The savings aren't as great as those from out-and-out discounters. And you usually have to ask for the concessions.

Once you have established a working relationship, keep monitoring the broker's performance. Has he been following your instructions, getting you quick execution of your orders and making no unauthorized transactions? Are his recommendations doing better—or worse—than the Standard & Poor Stock Index or the Dow-Jones Industrials? Is he churning your account—turning over your portfolio several times a year or running up commission costs that are a substantial fraction of your capital? If you feel that the performance is falling short, get yourself another broker!

The New York Stock Exchange has a number of pamphlets listing 300 member firms by region; they also give brief descriptions of the services each firm offers and minimum requirements for accounts. Write to the New York Stock Exchange, Public Information Office Directory, 11 Wall Street, New York, NY 10005, and ask for a pamphlet for your area.

Much of what has been said of brokers also applies to insurance agents who hold themselves out as financial planners. They, too, have products to sell— ordinary or whole life insurance, annuities, and the like. Their competence can range from considerable to judgments based largely on reading the same newspapers that you do. They frequently have literature and other material prepared by the home office, but as a rule it cannot compare in timeliness and sharp focus on specific situations with the research reports of a full-service brokerage. An insurance salesman isn't likely to have the breadth of background of a stockbroker, either—the knowledge of options or fixed-income securities, for example. As has been noted earlier, insurance is sold, not bought. If the agent doesn't happen to carry the kind of investment vehicle that would suit you best, it may never even be called to your attention.

Bank trust departments, which handle money of living persons as well as estates, are something else again. Their investment choices can range over a broad spectrum. What's more, you seldom have to worry about questions of integrity. And the bank performs many services that individuals often find a drag; it holds securities for safekeeping, handles purchases and sales, collects dividends and interest, and keeps records. Fees don't have to be high—1% or less of the assets being managed with minimums that depend on the kind of service you choose.

In the case of accounts that are managed for a single individual, the minimum could be $1,000 and even $2,000 or more. But many banks maintain pooled accounts which commingle the funds of many customers, much as in the case of a mutual fund. Minimum fees can range in the area of $250 to $500.

The trouble with bank trust departments is that their performance as managers has gen-

erally been mediocre. They have been intensely conservative. In their time-honored zeal to preserve the capital entrusted to them, they have been slow to move into newer—and not necessarily riskier—investment media. They have been slow in adjusting to changing climates and have shown earnings on money under their care that have lagged going rates. In this inflationary era, their conservatism has too often failed to increase capital in line with inflation; the result has been the very erosion in true capital values that their conservatism was designed to prevent.

During the Seventies, the value of bank pools of common stocks actually lagged the increase in share values generally—as measured by the Standard & Poor's index of 500 common stocks—by more than 10%. The banks didn't do nearly as well as the mutual funds, which outperformed stocks generally by a very comfortable margin.

To be sure, not all bank trust departments have been laggards. Every year, there seems to be a handful which performs handsomely, beating the mutual funds and even some of the consistently successful of the purist investment advisers. On the other hand, each year also brings some stories of gross mismanagement—stories of the sharp shrinkage in the value of funds under the bank's care. More recently, though, performance has been improving.

One final source of investment advice that's available to both do-it-yourselfers and to those who seek professional help is the numerous publications in the investment field—books, newsletters, magazines, and subscription services. Books seem to be a favored vehicle for the Doomsayers discussed in Chapter One—though they publish newsletters, too—while many more conventional authorities have also written books.

It is not too great an oversimplification to say that the books brought out in the past few years have typically—though by no means exclusively—pursued single themes as the basis for narrow and extreme investment recommendations. A major theme is the catastrophe in one form or another that is inevitable in just a short time—and how to prepare to profit from it. One might find the conclusions more believable if they were more consistent; in fact, though—except for a preponderant preference for gold— the specific advice may be wildly contradictory. These books may make interesting reading; if you buy their arguments, you won't have much need for any other kind of investment advice.

Newsletters provide a continuing source of somewhat less flamboyant recommendations than the books just alluded to. For prices ranging from well under $50 a year to as much as $500, you can get four or eight or more pages of advice on buying and selling every week (or fortnight or month). Some are mere tip sheets or vehicles for conveying the writer's theories of market performance. Others reflect careful research. But, despite claims of near-total infallibility, their records are rarely better than those of the investment advisers who talk to their clients directly.

Many of the newsletters on investments focus on technical analysis of market trends.(See Chapter Thirteen.) Their editors appeal to the investing public's hunger for the word on what's going to happen next. Some, like Joe Granville, are showmen with great charisma—and some competence as technical analysts. Granville takes credit for triggering a sharp stock-market break early in 1981, when he flashed the word to his telephone-service clients to "sell the market—sell everything." The fact is, though, that some other analysts were noting that the market was due for a correction before Granville gave the word—as some experts who stress fundamental (or real-world) factors were doing, too; indeed, many of these were in print while Granville was still trumpeting a bull market. Fast-moving speculators were already shifting their money elsewhere.

Unquestionably, though, well-known writers like Granville can be market forces unto themselves. Because of the size of their following and their reputations for being right, their pronouncements can—over the short-term—become self-fulfilling prophecies. Experience has shown, though, that the typical investor has neither the time, the resources, nor the aptitude to capitalize on the advice that technicians generate—nor the appetite for taking the risks of being wrong. He consistently does better when he buys for the longer pull; over time, he would have little regret that he didn't rush to buy or sell on the strength of a technician's urgent recommendations.

This is not to say that none of the investment letters is worthwhile. Some of the better, less shrill services can alert readers to developing trends that a subscriber might otherwise miss. The letters do some of the homework—analyzing the data on companies, industries or basic economic trends—that investors don't do for themselves.

When their recommendations are not hedged to the point of meaninglessness, they are often wrong as to timing of the predicted moves and even the direction. As with the case of specialists at brokerage houses, the specialized letters—dealing with some segment of the business like, say, options—may be more useful than the general run, not so much for their specific recommendations as their reports and analyses of what is going on in the area.

Services such as the Value Line Investment Survey (Arnold Bernhard & Co., 5 E. 44th Street, New York, NY 10017, annual subscription: $285) are relatively light on recommendations and jammed with statistical information on stocks and industries. Similarly, Forbes Magazine (60 Fifth Avenue, New York, NY 10011, annual subscription: $27) can be valuable for its updates on corporate developments, investment trends and annual surveys of corporate and mutual-fund performance.